FACE to FACE

A Sourcebook of Individual Consultation Techniques for Faculty/Instructional Developers

Karron G. Lewis, Ph.D. — *Editor*

and

Joyce T. Povlacs, Ph.D. — *Associate Editor*

NEW FORUMS PRESS, INC.
Stillwater, Oklahoma 74076

Library of Congress Catalog Card Number Pending

ISBN: 0-913507-08-3

This book is available at a special discount when ordered in bulk quantities. For information, contact New Forums Press, Inc., P.O. Box 876, Stillwater, OK 74076.

Printed in the United States of America.

Foreword

Over the years most faculty and instructional development programs have offered periodic workshops, discussion groups on a variety of teaching issues, written materials describing different teaching strategies, and other such services. However, most of us who have been in this business awhile have found that the best way to instill *lasting* commitment and change in a faculty member's teaching is through one-to-one consultation.

As you may expect, just as there are many different teaching methods and styles there are also numerous strategies which may be used in individual consultation. The purpose of this book is to explore some of the various individual consultation methods currently in use and through descriptive case studies enable you, the reader, to utilize or adapt one or more of these methods to your own consulting program.

Our aim is to serve both novice and experts alike. If you have just taken on the role of an instructional consultant—perhaps moving from a fulltime teaching position to do so—we hope you find a framework for your consultation, some new concepts to stimulate your thinking about it, and some specific methods which you can use to assist your colleagues in improving the teaching and learning on your campus. If you're an expert—well who is that person, anyway? Better, if you're a *veteran* (as each of us is—Karron, with fourteen years' experience, Joyce, with twelve), we invite you to discover, as we did, new ideas and approaches for conducting individual consultation in faculty and instructional development on our campuses.

We invite you to browse and to discover what is useful to you. As the contents of the articles and the credentials of their authors indicate, the strength of those doing consultation in faculty and instructional development in higher education lies in the group's diversity. We bring from the humanities, social sciences, natural sciences, and professional studies multiple perspectives and methods of inquiry. We hope that the variety of approaches represented here enhances your professional development as it has ours.

Perhaps as you read you will jot down notes or carry on "marginal" conversations with us. Feel free to contact the authors of the respective chapters to obtain additional information if just reading about their technique does not give you all the specifics you feel you need in order to use it.

We also encourage you to let us know whether the information contained in this book is useful and whether the case studies provided an adequate illustration of each technique. If you have a method or a strategy you feel you use successfully and it was not included in this volume, please send us a brief description of it for possible inclusion in a second volume.

Your comments and suggestions may be sent to Karron Lewis, Center for Teaching Effectiveness, Main Building 2200, The University of Texas at Austin, Austin, TX 78712-1111.

As with the production of any large project such as this, there are numerous individuals who make the final product a reality (in addition to the chapter contributors). First, we want to thank our many, many faculty colleagues who over the years have helped us hone our methods and who constantly keep us mindful of the complexities of teaching. We also want to thank Doug Dollar of New Forums Press, Inc. for his encouragement and guidance in the production of this book as well as J.D. Lewis (Karron's spouse) for the use of the Mac and laser printer at St. Edward's University which were used to create the camera-ready copy. And, finally, we thank our respective co-workers, Delivee Wright at University of Nebraska-Lincoln and Jim Stice and Marilla Svinicki at the University of Texas at Austin, for their patience and support through the extended process of getting this book into print.

Karron G. Lewis, Editor   *Joyce T. Povlacs, Associate Editor*
The University of Texas at Austin   University of Nebraska-Lincoln

Contents

Part I:
General Skills and Philosophies

The way in which you approach individual consultation can determine whether or not you will be successful. As a consultant, you join the ranks of those who provide professional services *and* who are truly concerned about the client. Dee Fink, in the first chapter in this section, shows this consultant-client relationship by comparing it to the work of a county agricultural extension agent. He focuses on six important elements coming from this comparison which are involved in the establishment of an effective program of instructional consulting.

The second chapter by Karron Lewis is an overview of individual consultation and why this is such an important part of most faculty development programs. It contains a discussion of the skills needed, places to find prospective clients, and a list of resources to tap for additional information.

In many ways, individual consultation is very much like doing research: you need to identify the question, collect data, analyze the data, interpret the data, and translate the data. In the third chapter by Jody Nyquist and Donald Wulff, this similarity to research is developed further and then applied in a case study.

Data collection, analysis, and evaluation are very important aspects of a successful consulting program. In the fourth chapter of this section, Jody Nyquist and Donald Wulff discuss the collection of *qualitative* data to describe what happens in complex university teaching environments. Because this data provides the foundation for your discussions with your faculty clients, it is imperative that this data be verifiable, valid and reliable. This paper should give you an excellent starting place as you begin thinking about data collection.

These chapters should provide a good general foundation for understanding the specific methodologies which are described in Parts II and III.

County Agents and Instructional Consultants: Tips on Establishing a Successful Consulting Program

L. Dee Fink
Office of Instructional Services
University of Oklahoma

When the editor of this collection of essays on instructional consulting approached me about contributing to the project, I was flattered, excited, and intimidated. The latter reaction was a result of my having been uneasy for some time about not having a more formalized approach to individual consulting sessions with faculty members. Basically, I try to listen well, and then make an intelligent and creative response. Although at times I still believe a good theory of teaching and consulting would be useful, this ad hoc approach has been at least modestly effective. A number of professors have been able to change their teaching practices in ways that made students react more positively to their classes and that allowed the professors themselves to feel more effective as teachers.

As a result of seeing my own approach to consulting as somewhat amorphous, I had difficulty coming up with a clear answer to the editor's question of: "*What* do you do as a consultant?" However, thinking about this question prompted me to think more extensively about the whole consulting process and, eventually, to develop an answer to a different question: "*Why* do I do what I do as a consultant?"

When a person sets up a program like this based on intuition rather than on the observation of many successful programs, it usually means the person is using a model that exists in their subconscious. So I tried to dig through my buried memories to see what I had been using as a model for my consulting program.

As it turns out, I carried this task with me through the end of the academic year and into the summer vacation. This year my family and I took our customary trip to a vacation trailer which we have set up on the family farm in rural Illinois. This is the farm where I grew up as a young boy and which I inherited a few years ago.

While there, I continued to ponder the question of how I developed the kind of consultation program that I did at the University of Oklahoma. At first, the question was not easy to answer. I had never had a course on instructional consulting, nor had I previously worked in a consulting program at another university.

Suddenly it dawned on me that I had probably been using, as a model, the role of the county agricultural extension agent which I had experienced as a boy growing up on this farm. The similarities between the roles and situations of the county extension agent and the instructional consultant are strong and clear. The county agent is supposed to help farmers improve their farming practices. There are many farmers in the county; they are more or less autonomous as farmers; they have nothing other than self-interest to motivate them to seek or accept the advice of the county agent. The instructional consultant is supposed to help teachers improve their teaching practices. There are many teachers in the college; they are more or less autonomous as teachers; and they have nothing more than self-interest to motivate them to seek or accept the advice of an instructional consultant.

After noting these similarities, I decided to pursue the comparison more extensively to see if it would shed any light on the question of how to establish a successful consulting role and program. Since the national agriculture extension service has been operating a consulting program for several decades with considerable success, the chance of acquiring some insight seemed quite good.

Also, rather fortuitously, I learned that the local county agent in this part of Illinois was retiring at this time. This led to an interview with him that took place on the last day before he retired; he had been a county agent for thirty years. Consequently he was in an excellent position and mood to give some informed thought to the question of how to succeed in a consulting role.

Establishing a Consulting Role

The following ideas and examples about consulting are the combined result of my own observations of county extension agents, my reflection on being an instructional consultant, and this county agent's thoughts on being an extension agent. These diverse threads of thought have been woven together into a tapestry that identifies six critical elements which need to be addressed when establishing a consulting program.

Role Identity

The first question that any consultant must address is the one of role identity. Who do you want to be—as a consultant? Every consultant carries in his or her head, consciously or unconsciously, an image of what a good consultant is like, that is, a role ideal. When articulated, this image might have the characteristics of a "superman" or "superwoman" who performs miracles, or it might be more akin to a doctor who can fix "sick fields" or "sick teachers," or the consultant might want to be "just like other farmers" or "teachers," except that they have a bit more technical training and therefore can answer some technical questions. The point here is that the role ideal can be defined in very different ways, each with its own justification. But, however it is defined, it will have a major influence on the self expectations and behavior of the person fulfilling the role.

As a young person growing up on the farm, I viewed the county agents as professional advisers: they were paid to be able to offer good advice to farmers. Furthermore, my image of the good ones (i.e., my image of their role ideal) was that they were both professionals and practitioners. That is, they operated their own farms in addition to being county agents. This made them more than "armchair farmers" and gave them much more credibility. In a related way, my image was also very clear about their dress code: from the waist up, they were professionals (that is, ironed shirt, tie when appropriate); from the waist down, they were practitioners (that is, trouser and shoes that would allow them to walk through barns or fields).

Similarly, I have defined my role as an instructional consultant in terms of being a professional adviser: I want to be able to offer good advice to teachers. In my mind, this requires that I too be both a professional and a practitioner. Consequently I have taken the time to continue teaching courses in my own discipline of origin (geography) in order to avoid being an armchair consultant. This practice has paid rich dividends in both the quality and credibility of my advice. Also, I very consciously changed my dress habits when I became a consultant. As a full-time faculty member, my attire tended to be on the casual side: I seldom wore a suit or tie. As a consultant, my role image calls for more emphasis on the professional part of my identity. Therefore I change my wardrobe and my dress habits accordingly: suit and tie become standard attire. My perception is that others have taken me more seriously since I began presenting myself as a serious professional.

These examples illustrate ways in which our role identity affects our self expectations and our behavior. But it also explains some of the problems that consultants can encounter. If one role image is along the lines of "being just like other farmers or teachers with a bit more technical training," expectations and productivity may be unnecessarily low. Over time, this perception can result in reduced support from the controlling organization. In a different way, if one's role identity is closer to being a "superman," self expectations may be too great and self evaluations therefore unnecessarily low. Again, over time, this perception would probably result in mental stress and poor self-esteem.

This analysis suggests that the whole question of role identity in fact involved three factors as indicated in the following diagram:

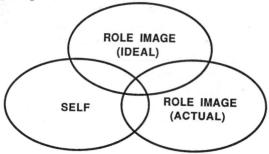

There should be some overlap between our self identity, our image of how we would ideally fulfill our roles, and our image of how we actually fulfill our roles. The degree to which the three factors coincide marks the extent to which we can experience personal satisfaction in fulfilling a role we consider valuable. But there also needs to be some separation between the three factors. We need to have a "sense of self" apart from our role; we also need a role ideal somewhat bigger and better than our actual role image, to leave room for growth.

My concluding point is that, as consultants, we need to give a lot of careful and conscious thought to how we define our role ideal. It exerts a major influence on what we do, on our ability to establish productive relationships with our would be clients, and affects the likelihood of our experiencing satisfaction (or disappointment) in this role.

Visibility

A second major part of consulting is creating and maintaining visibility. The county agent in Illinois said he prepared periodic mail-outs to farmers, had frequent spots on the county radio station, and wrote regular columns in the local newspapers. These activities were all intended to keep farmers in the area aware that his office did exist, who the person was that occupied that office, and what services were available there. If successful, these efforts increased the likelihood that the farmers would think of him and be willing to contact him when they had a question or problem in their farming operation.

But the agent also pointed out that he talked with non-farmers in the local community whenever he could. Organizations such as the Kiwanis, Rotary, and Chamber of Commerce frequently invited him to luncheon meetings. In this predominantly rural community, these people were keenly interested in the current situation of farmers and in their future prospects. The county agent was the person they turned to for that information.

In a similar way, the instructional consultant also needs to constantly work to maintain visibility. On my own campus, the primary means for doing this has been the publication of a four-page newsletter that goes to all faculty members and teaching assistants. It is published four times a year and includes vignettes of excellent teachers, summaries of national reports on college teaching, campus events affecting teaching, and descriptions of books and articles on teaching available through my office. Parenthetically I would add that enough time and money have been allocated to the preparation of the newsletter to give it a high quality, professional appearance. It is the one thing that every faculty member sees from my office; it should therefore create the expectations of receiving high quality, professional service if and when they decide to contact me for consulting services.

Also, as part of the visibility effort, I set up visits each fall with all new chairs and other new administrators. I visit them in their offices, explain the range of services available from my office, and leave a sheet of paper which describes my services and lists my name, phone number, and campus address. I make visits because of my belief that chairs are very important allies in encouraging faculty members who could benefit from my services to, in fact, use them. Therefore I want them to have a clear understanding of my services. But the visits also give the chairs a chance to evaluate me as the person fulfilling the consultant role, and I gain an impression of what the chair is like.

In terms of working with people other than teachers, I have not been as active as I could and should. The local radio station did invite me in for an interview once, and I have had formal visits with the directors of other units within the university, such as the Office of Student Affairs. But my favorite example of this kind of visibility comes from Texas A&M University. Consultants in the Center for Teaching Excellence there had the opportunity to talk with the members of the "Texas A&M Aggie Mother's Club," a very strong organization, about their efforts to help faculty members improve their teaching. As a result, this group spoke to high level administrators in the university about the possibility of getting more money to support an activity they thought would be very beneficial to their children who were students at the university.

But the importance of this activity for the consulting process is not just that it produces a steady supply of clients and perhaps enhances organizational support. It has been my observation that it also changes the consultant. As the result of preparing newsletters and talking to non-teachers about teachers and teaching, I find my own understanding and valuing of the act of teaching evolves.[1] This in turn affects what I am able to do and am ready to do in individual consulting sessions.

Program Development

Good consultants do not just sit by the phone and wait for clients to contact them; they need to develop a program of activities. Some of these, to be sure, will be "reactive" where they respond to client initiated contacts. But another major part of the program needs to be "proactive," that is, an activity initiated by the consultant.

A county agricultural agent sets up a series of seminars, workshops, and demonstration programs each year. These might include such things as a seminar by a college professor on growing alfalfa hay, a workshop by a local banker on setting up a proper cash flow system, or a demonstration day that involves visits to several farms showing how tool sheds are organized.

Similarly a good consulting program at a university needs a proactive dimension. In my own case, I have sponsored a few workshops (for example, an annual orientation program for new teaching assistants, one on computer assisted instruction, and another on preparing for the tenure review process). But the more important activity has been the formation of several faculty discussion groups each year. These are groups of fifteen or so faculty members who join a particular group for a year-long series of bi-weekly meetings and activities. Each group is involved in a different activity, and people choose which group they want to belong to. The specific thrust of the groups changes each year, but the following list of recent topics (each lasting a whole semester or a whole year) illustrates the variety and

---

[1]This is the same effect that writing an article like this has on a person. The process of developing a formal statement on a topic leads to major changes in one's original ideas on the subject.

flexibility that is possible in such an activity:

- inviting state leaders in to talk about the attitude of Oklahomans toward higher education,

- inviting students in to describe their views on what constitutes good teaching,

- teaching large classes,

- designing a new course,

- making better tests,

- using writing activities to promote better content learning,

- visiting and critiquing each others classroom teaching,

- visiting the classes of and talking with outstanding teachers on campus.

The value of having strong activities is both the reactive and proactive realms in that they complement each other. Sometimes a contact with a faculty member starts with a request for me to visit his or her classes and see if I can discern why they are getting low student evaluations. In the resulting conversation, I frequently suggest that the individual join a particular discussion group next semester or next year. Conversely, people sometimes join one of these groups on their own initiative and then, as a result of the attitudes and values supported by the group, find the courage to request my consulting service for individual attention to a teaching problem they have.

A final issue related to program development is the one of participation, ownership and control. Who participates, owns and controls the decisions about program development? It might be *the* instructional consultant, or a group of clients (that is, faculty members), or a group of higher administrators. There are pros and cons to each alternative. In my case, I have been the only one responsible for program development although I try to keep my ideas informed by careful listening and by informally soliciting ideas. For the past year or so, I have been trying to organize a campus-wide council on teaching, composed of faculty members from all colleges, that would identify (and hopefully be able to act on) institutional impediments to teaching as well as assist me in the determination of worthwhile program activities. Thus far I have not succeeded in convincing the Faculty Senate that it ought to add yet another service committee to the long list it already has (a problem which I understand and appreciate). But it is still on my agenda as something important in order to broaden participation and ownership in the instructional development program in this institution.

Communicating

One of the more light-hearted moments in my interview with the county agent came when I asked how he handled personal relationships with farmers. He said that most of the people in this area are German Dutch. Some of them want you to tell them exactly what to do. But with others, you "---- well" better not tell them what to do. And you have to figure out which kind of person you are talking to.

But with either kind of farmer, he took an "educational approach" to consulting: you find out what question the person has, you identify the options, and then lay out the pros and cons of each option.

For example, one farmer wanted to use a certain herbicide or weedkiller in his soybean field. The county agent looked up the legal restrictions on it and then told the farmer what they were. The herbicide would kill the grass in his soybean field but the soybeans themselves could not then be used to feed beef cattle or dairy cattle. The farmer then had to decide whether this was compatible with his plans for that crop, or whether he needed to use a different herbicide to get rid of the grass in his field.

In a different example, another farmer had decided, after noticing that hog prices were good, to expand into the hog business and requested advice about how to construct the hog buildings. The county agent wanted to warn the farmer that hog prices might well go down in the future, but he did not do so because the man had clearly already made up his mind to go into the hog business. Therefore the agent limited his advice to that requested: how to construct the building so as to be able to conform to EPA regulations on the disposal of manure, and so forth.

These examples illustrate the basic principles I try to follow as an instructional consultant. The first and most important requirement, when a faculty member comes to my office and requests help, is to *listen carefully*. I need to quickly determine both what kind of person I am dealing with and what it is they want—really. Some are quite straight forward and adept at indicating what they are looking for. With others, you have to "read between the lines" because they are unable or unwilling to say what their quest is really for.

Many simply want better student evaluations so they can get better departmental evaluations and higher pay raises. Others think their students are not learning well and want more effective methods of teaching. Yet others just do not *feel* good about their relationships with students and are looking for ways to change this feeling. Some do not have a particular teaching problem as such, but they are bored with using the same procedures for many years and want something new, different and more exciting for themselves. A few seem to want someone else to confirm that they are doing a good job (which they think they are) even though their students and/or their colleagues think otherwise. A consultant has to sort through all these possibilities in a relatively short time and usually indirectly, to determine what the client's real agenda is.

The second principle is not to over-respond. As with the county agent, I sometimes face the danger and temptation of telling clients more than they want to know. After visiting their classes, I may see a host of problems. But I have to select only one or two as the most important ones to start working on. Or, if someone comes to my office to ask if I have any material on leading better discussions and I have a file with seven different articles, I have to restrict myself to pulling only one or two that would be good for this client.

Occasionally I may see the need to change a person's agenda. One faculty member recently said his students were complaining about his lectures and asked if I had any material that would help him improve his lectures. Having visited the person's classes previously, I doubted whether he really had the ability to consistently give outstanding lectures. So instead, I raised the possibility of his redesigning his course to reduce the amount of time given over to lecturing and to replace it with small group activities. In this case, enough information was available to convince him it was worth a try and he spent the summer redesigning his course.

This deviation from the general principle of identifying and adhering to the client's agenda can work. But it should be used judiciously and only in those cases where the consultant knows the client would be open to a different agenda.

Gathering, Interpreting and Responding to Information

Once a consultant and a client have determined what question they want to work on, they next have to decide whether more information is needed and, if so, how to get it.

Farmers often come to the county agent and say, "I have a field that isn't producing well. What can I do about it?" The county agent's task is to help the farmer sort through several possible explanations and responses. One possibility is that the field is deficient in one of the basic fertilizers. A test for this condition can be easily obtained through the local fertilizer company. Another explanation is that the farmer is not using the right seed variety. The county agent can obtain the data from local test plots to determine the best kind of seed for the particular kind of soil in the field. Or it may be that the field lacks a critical trace mineral. Soil samples can be sent to the state extension service for this kind of information. The county agent's task, in such situations, is to know what the possible explanations for the problem are, what information is needed to assess each hypothesis, and how to obtain the necessary information.

My responsibilities are the same when a faculty member comes to me and says, "I have a class that isn't going very well. What can I do about it?" In some cases, I may be able to give an answer right away, based on information I already have about this particular situation or about teaching in general. But in many cases, I will have to decide what

additional information would be appropriate: a classroom
visit, a careful look at course materials, videotaping the class,
administering a questionnaire to the class, or interviewing
some students.

Once the information has been obtained, it has to be
interpreted. This is often not easy. For example, the holistic
information from classroom visits or videotapes can be
interpreted in many ways. I tend to ask the following kinds of
questions:

- First, what is happening here? Is the teacher trying to
  inform, persuade, excite, give practice, develop self-
  confidence, or what?

- Second, how good and how bad are particular events? Is
  the teacher succeeding moderately well or very well in
  giving real-life examples of a concept? Are the discussion
  questions somewhat or very closed-ended?

- Third, what is the relative importance of different events?
  Is the passivity of the students' role in this class more
  important than the fact that the teacher does not know their
  names, or vice versa?

- Fourth, what interaction effects are occurring? I may
  conclude that, yes, the teacher is a bit surly, but this is
  partly because several students really are obnoxious.

Finally, once the information has been interpreted, the
client and consultant have to decide how to respond to it. It
may call for the teacher to improve a particular skill (for
example, giving more organized lectures), or changing the
design of the course (for example, more group activities
rather than lectures), or making a procedural adaptation (for
example, learning students' names and having them sit closer
together so they will be more responsive to questions asked by
the teacher). The consultant also has to decide what role to
play in the response phase. The response may involve
providing written information, coaching the person, inviting
him or her to participate in a workshop or discussion group,
or referring the person to observe or talk with another faculty
member.

Maintaining Quality Performance Over Time

Any consultant who wants to engage in this activity over an extended period of time must give some thought to the question of how to maintain the quality of his or her performance. In my mind, this calls for three kinds of responses:

* continuing to learn about the field in general,
* keeping abreast of resources and changes in the local setting, and
* developing additional skills and competencies.

For county agents, the need to learn about general changes in agriculture has been a major task. In just a few decades, they have seen numerous and rapid innovations in the farming scene, as, for example, the introduction of hybrid seeds, commercial fertilizers, chemical herbicides and pesticides, and a mountain of research on the effectiveness of alternative farming techniques. In addition to this information, they have had to "know the territory." County agents must be familiar with: local levels of production (and how these have varied over time and from place to place), which farmers are trying what new techniques and with what results, key resource people both within the farming population and the broader community, the activities of related organizations such as the Farm Bureau and Future Farmers of America, etc. Finally, they had to learn new skills and competencies. This learning includes trying some of the new farming practices as well as learning soil testing procedures, communication skills with individual farmers, public speaking, and so on.

The instructional consultant has a parallel set of learning responsibilities. *First*, I feel a need to keep up with published material offering new ideas both on teaching itself and on instructional development programs, research reports on the same topics, new testing procedures, national reports critiquing higher education, and so forth. *Second*, I try to know locally which teachers are trying what new techniques and with what results, how teaching is evaluated in different academic units, new administrative policies affecting teaching, changes in the character of the student population, new resource people (both within the faculty and within the broader academic community), and so forth. *Finally,* there are several skills and competencies that I work on over time. I like to be personally familiar with innovative teaching activities (for example, small groups, writing exercises to promote content learning, computer-assisted instruction). I am always trying to improve my "eye-ball" knowledge, that is, the ability to observe a teacher in the classroom and identify important strengths and weaknesses. In addition, the basic skills of listening and communicating well with teachers (and others) are practices that need continuous honing to keep sharp.

The degree to which I succeed or fail in these three parts of my continuing professional education affects essentially every new consulting case I have.

Conclusions

This chapter has described one person's view of six important elements involved in the establishment of an effective program of instructional consulting. In general terms, these can be summarized as:

1. defining the consulting role in terms that are congruent with one's own personality and yet are anchored in a challenging role ideal,

2. maintaining visibility with intended clients but also with people in a broader range of related roles,

3. developing a program that has a strong proactive as well as reactive dimension,

4. learning to communicate well which, among other things, means knowing how to discern the kind of person one is talking to, how to read between the lines of what they are saying, and knowing when to shut up,

5. being able to gather, interpret, and respond to information about client-defined problems, and

6. continuing the professional education process which is necessary to stay alive and vital as a consultant.

Hopefully, this parallel look at another consulting role, the county agricultural agent, has been not only enjoyable but informative. My own view is that teaching has a lot in common with the activity of farming. Hence the kind of consulting done by county agents is more similar to instructional consulting than, say, a financial advisor or a medical doctor. To the degree that this is true, a close look at the county agent can make us more conscious of aspects of our own work in higher education than we otherwise would be.

To close this chapter, I would like to share the comments of the county agent I interviewed when he following question: "What advice would you give to a person just starting their career in this field?"

His answer was as follows, "First, you have to learn how to sell yourself to others. To do this, you have to believe in what you are doing. Second, you have to have some initiative to learn about farming and about farmers. Third, you have to be exciting when you're talking about what you are doing. Fourth, you need to make other people feel good about themselves. And finally: Don't bluff! Try to know as much as you can; but when you don't know, be honest about it."

Not bad advice for a new instructional consultant as well!

L. Dee Fink is an Instructional Consultant in the Office of Instructional Services and an Assistant Professor of Geography at the University of Oklahoma. His academic background is in Geography and he has been in Faculty Development related activities since 1979. His is essentially a one-person operation, but he has been able to spread his influence over most of the campus with his innovative programs. He may be reached at: Office of Instructional Services, Carnegie Building, Room 116, University of Oklahoma, Norman, OK 73019. (405) 325-3521.

Individual Consultation: Its Importance to Faculty Development Programs

Karron G. Lewis
Center for Teaching Effectiveness
The University of Texas at Austin

For a majority of the people in faculty and instructional development the most time-consuming, yet most rewarding, activity is consulting with faculty members on a one-to-one basis. Through this type of individual work with faculty members, we are able to focus on each person's strengths and concerns to facilitate discovery of alternative teaching methods, better testing methods, confidence in themselves as public speakers, or whatever will help each one do a more effective job as a faculty member in an institution of higher education.

As you might expect, there are many different techniques which may be used in the individual consultation process as well as some essential skills which consultants need to cultivate. In this chapter I would like to share some of these techniques and skills with you and give you some additional resources to look at if you run into difficulties.

Why Engage in Individual Consultation?

One of the primary goals of most faculty/instructional development programs is to help faculty members become more productive and happier members of the higher education community. Because very few graduate degree programs provide instruction in "how" to teach the content, a majority

Adapted, with minor changes, from a chapter found in *Professional and organizational development: A handbook for practitioners* edited by Emily C. Wadsworth.

of the faculty development programs which are currently in operation focus on helping faculty members learn how to teach more effectively (Erickson, 1986). Most programs offer periodic workshops during which a variety of teaching skills and techniques are demonstrated and discussed, but over the years I have found that the best way to instill *lasting* commitment and change is through one-to-one consultation.

Where Do Clients Come From?

Potential clients for one-to-one consultation consist of *all* of the faculty members on your campus. However, getting them to contact you for individual assistance may be difficult until you have "proven" yourself. This proof often begins in campus-wide workshops where you demonstrate your competence and get to know the faculty members. Additional proof comes after you have had a chance to work individually with some faculty members and they "spread the word" that you don't bite and can actually provide useful information and assistance.

My individual clients usually come from three sources: 1) university-wide conferences and workshops, 2) former clients telling others about our services, and 3) the student Course-Instructor Evaluations.

University-wide Conferences/Workshops. Each year in August our Center conducts a three-day Teaching-Orientation Seminar for New Faculty and in January we host a two-day Experienced Faculty Teaching Conference. Many of my new clients now say that because they got to know me during these activities, they feel comfortable asking me for assistance when they run into a teaching problem.

Former Clients. Many of my new clients also indicate that they decided to contact me because a friend of theirs recommended our services. It helps that our success rate has been quite high over the years (i.e., the clients' student ratings have improved, the clients feel better about themselves and their teaching, the clients have won teaching awards, and so forth), but former clients are typically one of our best sources of publicity.

Instructor-Course Evaluations. On our campus the student evaluation of a course/instructor is voluntary in most departments. In the past few years, however, the administration has begun to emphasize that proof of teaching effectiveness must be submitted for tenure and promotion decisions. This emphasis has provided the impetus for faculty members with low student ratings to seek our assistance.

As you can see, faculty members will come if you make yourself and your programs visible and, once you experience success with a few faculty members, word will spread rather quickly.

Individual Consultation Techniques:
The Many Hats of the Consultant

We all know from learning theory that motivation and relevance are both necessary for effective learning to take place. Thus, the task of the consultant is to help the client (faculty member) think about what is happening in his or her teaching and develop some alternate strategies for dealing with the problems. As you work with each individual case, you, as the consultant, must wear a number of different hats.

Consultant as Data Collector. To focus the client's thoughts on what is currently happening in his/her classroom, you need to collect data which describe the activities and highlight the affect of these activities on the students. This may consist of:

1. *conducting a pre-observation interview* to determine why the faculty member is seeking assistance and what might be the best course of action to follow. During this interview you will probably collect a variety of data such as:

   a. a description of his or her class(es) — verbal and via the written syllabus for the course;
   b. the specific types of feedback the faculty member is seeking (for example, Are my lectures organized? Am I responding adequately to student questions?);
   c. the faculty member's attitude toward students and teaching;
   d. any personal things which may be affecting his/her professional activities (for example, a new baby or over-commitment on committees);.

e. any other information which relates to the client's request for assistance.

2. *analysis and evaluation of course materials* (for example, syllabus, objectives, assignments, exams, texts) to help you and the client determine whether or not the goals for student learning are clearly stated and whether appropriate teaching strategies are being used;

3. *sitting in on two or three of the class sessions* to determine the pace, the organization of the content, the activities of the students during class, the amount and what types of interaction take place between the teacher and students (through the use of observation instruments such as the Cognitive Interaction Analysis System — Lewis & Johnson, 1986), attentiveness of students during class, and so forth;

4. *relating previous student evaluation data* to the in-class observation;

5. *soliciting early feedback from the students* through written or verbal evaluations — such as the use of small group feedback (Clark & Bekey, 1979) or TABS (Bergquist & Phillips, 1975);

6. *video or audiotaping a class session* for analysis by you and the teacher;

7. and anything else which will facilitate the in-depth analysis and evaluation of the course and the way it is being taught.

Consultant as Data Manager. Once you have collected the data which you feel will be most helpful in your analysis of this client's concerns, then you must be able to arrange this data in such a way that the faculty member can relate what he or she is currently doing to what he or she would like to do. Since many of the educational concepts (which may be very familiar to us as consultants) are foreign to many faculty members, coming up with ways to make the data "real" may be a challenge. I have found that graphs and other "visual" (as opposed to "cognitive" or "prose") presentations of evaluation data, in-class interactions, and such can be grasped much more rapidly than several paragraphs explaining the theory or main ideas behind a particular teaching technique.

For example, if the instructor is concerned that only a few of the students are really taking part in the analysis of the cases being studied in class, you might use a diagram of where the students are seated in class and then each time one of them speaks, place a tally mark in his or her box. In addition, it is often enlightening to draw arrows to designate "to whom" the student is directing his or her comments. Then tally marks may be made along that arrow when such interactions occur again (see **Figure 1**). Of course, the size of the class is a limiting factor in this type of data collection, but it provides a very clear picture of what is happening. If the data show that there are just a few people participating and they are always directing their comments back to the teacher, then the instructor, probably with a little assistance from you, can develop some strategies for involving a larger number of students in the discussion process.

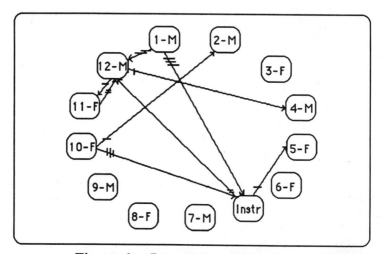

Figure 1.   Interaction Diagram

Consultant as Facilitator. One of the most important hats you wear in individual consultation is that of a facilitator. Once the data have been gathered and arranged in an understandable format, you will probably sit down with the faculty member and discuss what you observed. At this point you should try not to make any suggestions or judgments about the effectiveness or non-effectiveness of the way things are currently being done. This is often difficult! Rather, your role is to encourage the instructor to talk about what he/she hoped would happen during the class session, what actually happened, and what might have been done differently to make the students grasp the essence of the lesson more easily.

In order for the instructor to actually *do* something to change what happened in the classroom, the "ownership" of the consultation process must be with him or her, not with the consultant (Nyquist, 1986; Taylor-Way, 1987). Thus, you should facilitate the brainstorming of ideas and alternative techniques, not present a ready-made list to the client. You do, however, help keep the actual changes which are attempted to a manageable number.

You can also encourage the client to start with things which require the fewest drastic revisions and then progress to more radical ideas. For example, try to discourage completely changing a course from straight lecture to *all* case studies. Incorporating one or two case studies to illustrate concepts discussed in the lecture would probably be more reasonable. Then, if those case studies go well, add additional case studies and maybe other types of group work to help the students relate the material to real problems.

Consultant as Support System. Once the instructor has, with your assistance, determined what needs to be done to make his or her teaching more effective, then you become his or her support system. Many times, the first attempt to incorporate something new into one's teaching winds up not changing anything or, even more traumatic, making things worse. At this point, you need to help the client analyze what parts of the change actually did go well and why the new technique didn't bring all of the expected results. Be as positive as possible!

It is often helpful if you can be in the class when these new techniques are being tried out. Then, you will have first-hand knowledge of what the instructor actually did, not reliance on his or her memory of what took place. Frequently, things are much worse in our memory than they were in reality. An audio or videotape of the class session might also be very helpful if it wouldn't be distracting to the instructor. Some instructors want to "try out" a new technique privately and then, when they feel comfortable, request an observation or videotape be made. You have to judge which would be most appropriate for each particular client.

Consultant as Counselor. Not infrequently, problems which faculty members are having in their classrooms stem from personal or professional stresses. Because being a faculty member takes so much of one's time and energy, it is not uncommon for family problems to arise. If a faculty member is going through a divorce or has a child who is having problems in school or is rebellious, these stresses affect his or her ability to concentrate on teaching and the preparation which is necessary for doing it well. I'm not saying that you should try to solve these problems unless, of course, you have training in counseling. However, you need to be alert to the possibility of these things influencing the performance of a client. If you feel you can't handle the problem, consult a professional who may help you decide whether or not professional expertise is needed, or you can encourage your client to consult someone.

For example, I had a client — a third-year faculty member — who had become over committed in the department, was in charge of a major committee in his professional organization, and his wife, who was also working, was expecting their second child (the first child was currently in kindergarten). On top of this, he was teaching three courses with extensive labs. Needless to say, his student evaluations plummeted and he was frantic when he called me. In this case, we were able to determine that his problem was an inability to be assertive and say "no." There wasn't much we could do about that particular semester, but we talked about assertiveness and role played some typical situations in which he found himself. Then, to manage the rest of that semester, we worked on some time management techniques and relaxation techniques which might help him cope with the tension and stress he was continually feeling. Happily, he made it through that semester. The next semester he had managed to reduce his departmental commitments (that is, committees) and he was no longer chairing the committee in his professional organization. Consequently, his student

evaluations returned to their previous highs and he was able to
enjoy life (and the new addition to their family) a little more.

Consultant as Information Source. If you and your
client have decided to incorporate a new technique into his or
her repertoire, it is useful to provide articles or chapters
which describe the technique and give case studies showing
how it has been used. If possible, provide copies of the actual
articles, not just a reference for the client to find for
him/herself. Remember, time is a valuable commodity for a
faculty member. In fact, if the articles are extremely long, the
inclusion of a brief abstract is almost essential. Otherwise, the
client will not be enthusiastic about wading through many
pages. After these have been read, sit down with your client
and discuss the articles, clarifying any words or concepts
which were unclear and relating how this can be adapted for
use in his or her classroom.

Most of the time these "new" techniques come from
keeping up with the current teaching literature, from trying
new things myself, or from observing someone else use a
particular technique. Because most faculty members tend to
teach as they were taught, the lecture mode predominates.
However, the learning literature shows that active students
learn more and retain it longer, so one of my main objectives
is frequently to encourage more student participation. Some
of the references I provide which focus on these "new"
student-oriented techniques are:

1. *Lecture/Discussion Techniques -*

   a. Osterman, D., Christiansen, M. and the late Coffey, B. (1985).
      The feedback lecture. *Idea Paper,* No. 13, January, Kansas
      State University, Center for Faculty Evaluation and
      Development.

   b. Woods, J.D. (1983). Lecturing: Linking purpose and
      organization. *Improving College and University Teaching,
      31,* (2), 61-64.

   c. Bowman, J.S. (1979). The lecture-discussion format revisited.
      Improving College and University Teaching, 27, (1), 25-27.

2. Small Group Techniques -

a. Bazeli, F.P. (1978). Learning team approach to large group instruction. *Improving College and University Teaching, 26,* (3), 201-202.

b. Bouton, C. and Garth, R. (eds.) (1983). Learning in Groups, *New Directions for Teaching and Learning, 14,* San Francisco: Jossey-Bass, Inc.

c. Collier, K.G. (1980). Peer-group learning in higher education: The development of higher order skills. *Studies in Higher Education, 5,* 55-62.

d. Haber, M.J. (1979). Increasing class participation using small groups. *Clearing House, 52,* 295-297.

e. Hoover, K. (1980). Small group techniques. In *College teaching today: A handbook for postsecondary instruction.* Boston: Allyn and Bacon, Inc., 65-83.

f. Hunsaker, J.S. and Roy, W. (1977). The group-centered classroom: Alternative to individualized instruction? *Educational Leadership, 34,* 366-369.

3. *Utilizing Effective Questioning Strategies* (for Discussions and Case Studies)

a. Hoover, K. (1980). Questioning strategies. In *College teaching today: A handbook for postsecondary instruction.* Boston: Allyn and Bacon, Inc., 101-119. (See also chapters "Discussion Methods," pp.120-149; "Analyzing Reality: The Case Method," pp.199-223.)

b. Lewis, K.G. Developing questioning skills. An unpublished handout available from the Center for Teaching Effectiveness, Main Building 2200, The University of Texas at Austin, Austin, TX 78712-1111.

c. Lewis, K.G. Evaluating discussion. An unpublished handout available from the Center for Teaching Effectiveness, Main Building 2200, The University of Texas at Austin, Austin, TX 78712-1111.

d. Watkins, K. (1983). Handling difficult questions and situations. *Innovation Abstracts, 5,* (24), available from National Institute for Staff and Organizational Development, EDB 348, The University of Texas at Austin, Austin, TX 78712-1111.

   e. Worsley, A.F. (1975). Improving classroom discussions: Ten
       principles. *Improving College and University Teaching, 23,*
       (1), 27.

4. *Why Get Students Involved?* (To help faculty understand *why*
students need to be actively involved in their learning.)

   a. Svinicki, M.D. Some applied learning theory. An unpublished
       handout available from the Center for Teaching Effectiveness,
       Main Building 2200, The University of Texas at Austin,
       Austin, TX 78712-1111.

   b. Svinicki, M.D. & Dixon, N.M. (1987). Kolb model modified for
       classroom activities. *College Teaching, 35,* (4), 141-146.

   c. Kolb, D.A. (1984). *Experiential learning: Experience as the
       source of learning and development.* Englewood Cliffs, New
       Jersey: Prentice-Hall.

Thus, as you can see, the role of the consultant in the
individual consultation process is constantly changing. But, in
order for us to provide this service to our clients, we need to
be flexible and willing to let the client make most of the
decisions.

Skills Needed for Individual Consultation

As with any profession, there are a number of skills
which will make you more effective in your job. Faculty
development is no different. Those which seem to be most
essential in our profession are listed and discussed briefly
below:

• *Listening* — This is perhaps the **most important** skill because you
will be doing a lot of it — when talking to your clients, when observing
classes, when obtaining verbal student evaluations, and so forth. If you
have trouble listening and concentrating on what is being said, this may
be a skill you need to work on.

• *Data collection* —I'm sure you have done quite a bit of this in your
quest for your own educational goals. However, collecting *qualitative*
rather than *quantitative* data may not have been addressed in your course
of study. If this is the case, you may wish to read more about this (see
listings in the **Additional Reading** at the end of this chapter).

- *In-class observation skills* — What kinds of things are important to student learning in a class of 500? Are these drastically different from the things which are important in a class of 50? or 15? Learning to attend to the important things in an in-class observation and leaving out the unimportant is also a skill. During my first in-class observation for a client I try to be a typical student: I take notes, may read or do the assignment prior to class, try to make sense of the lecture, write down questions which came to mind (I seldom ask questions in a class because it usually makes the teacher very nervous), and so forth. In addition, if obvious problems are noticed (e.g., the writing on the overhead transparency is too small to read), I jot those down in the margins. It is also helpful if you and the client can determine one or two things he or she would like you to look for during the observation. This will help focus your observation as well as your later discussions about that class session. Use of check sheets, evaluation forms, or an objective observation system are also helpful in this respect. (See Bergquist and Phillips, 1975 & 1977.)

- *Ability to facilitate analysis of data by faculty member* — Just as you may be unfamiliar with the techniques and results of collecting qualitative data, your clients may also have difficulty understanding anything without definite numbers attached. The key to facilitating this understanding is for you to be as objective as possible when collecting the data. Use of observation systems such as the *Cognitive Interaction Analysis System* (Lewis & Johnson, 1986) can help make your explanation of the interactions which took place in the class much easier to understand and provides a concrete means for assessing change. (See **Additional Reading** section for more information.)

- *Positive reinforcement* — This skill is quite difficult for many people in higher education because they have spent so much time criticizing journal articles, others' research studies, their own writing, and so on, that it may be hard to focus on the positive aspects of a client's teaching and written output. In addition, you may sometimes get a client who is *really* ineffective and finding something good to say to get things started may take a lot of skill in this area. You may want to practice by first, writing down all of the words and phrases which you consider reinforcing (e.g., good job, excellent, yes, you're on the right track). Then, audiotape one of your own classes and notice what you do to reinforce your students for correct answers, good questions, good behavior, and so forth. If your reinforcement vocabulary is limited, try to expand it. If you tend to criticize more than you reinforce, try looking for positive things first and then move to constructive criticism.

- *Empathy* — If you have been a faculty member this shouldn't be a problem for you. However, by pooling your resources with your client and by using the POD Network (colleagues in professional and organizational development who belong to the Professional and Organizational Development Network in Higher Education), you will probably be able to resolve most problems which you encounter. (For information about this organization and membership requirements, contact Karron Lewis.)

• *Keeping up with the literature of faculty development and teaching* — Knowledge of learning theory, motivation theory, teaching techniques for a variety of classes and situations, data collection instruments, questioning skills, empathy . . . there is a lot to get familiar with if you plan to do a good job as a consultant. See the following section for some suggested resources.

Though this may seem like a lot to keep up with, you probably already have many of these skills at some proficiency level. Once you have consulted with a few clients you will find that it is a wonderful experience and any specific knowledge you may need to help a client can usually be acquired with a trip to the library, or by calling one of your POD colleagues. The real key, on your part, is a desire to help a fellow faculty member find enrichment and fulfillment in becoming a more effective instructor.

Resources to Tap for Additional Information

POD Members - This is probably your *most valuable resource.* Call them and be sure to Network with them at the Annual Conference.

Newsletters from Faculty/Instructional Development Centers - most Centers will exchange newsletters with you free of charge.

Other Journals and Publications -
• *To Improve the Academy* - Annual publication of POD
      Network available to all members free of charge.
• *College Teaching* - Published quarterly by Heldref
      Publications, 4000 Albemarle St., NW,
      Washington, D.C. 20016
• *Higher Education Abstracts* - Published quarterly by The
      Claremont Graduate School, 740 No. College Ave.,
      Claremont, CA 91711
• Teaching journals in various fields - (e.g., *Teaching
      Sociology, Engineering Education,* etc.)
• ERIC Publications

* *New Directions in Teaching and Learning* - series by Jossey-Bass, Publishers
* *Handbook for Faculty Development* -Vols. 1,2 & 3, Bergquist and Phillips (See complete citation in reference section.)

Attendance at professional meetings - Most discipline-specific professional organizations have a special interest group which includes members who are interested in studying the most effective techniques for teaching the discipline. You could be a valuable resource for this group and you could also discover additional ideas to pass along to your faculty clients by interacting with these colleagues.

References

Bergquist, W.H. & Phillips, S.R. (1975, 1977, and 1981). *A handbook for faculty development*. Vol. 1, 2 & 3. Washington, D.C.: Council for the Advancement of Small Colleges.

Clark, J. & Bekey, J. (1979). Use of small groups in instructional evaluation. *POD Quarterly. 1*, 87-95.

Erickson, G. (1986). A survey of faculty development practices. *To Improve the Academy, 5* , 182-196.

Lewis, K. & Johnson, G.R. (1986). *Monitoring your classroom communication skills: A programed workbook for developing coding skills using Johnson's cognitive interaction analysis system (CIAS) and expanded CIAS.* Unpublished programed workbook and audiotape for skill training in CIAS. Distributed by: The Center for Teaching Effectiveness, Main Building 2200, The University of Texas at Austin, Austin, TX 78712-1111.

Nyquist, J.D. (1986). CIDR: A small service firm within a research university. *To improve the academy, 5,* 66-83. Professional & Organizational Development Network in Higher Education and National Council for Staff Program and Organizational Development. Stillwater, OK: New Forums Press.

Taylor-Way, David (in press). Consultation with video: Memory management through stimulated recall. In K.G. Lewis & J.T. Povlacs (eds.), *Face to face: A sourcebook of individual consultation techniques for faculty development personnel*. Stillwater, OK: New Forums Press.

Additional Reading

Allen, D.W. & Ryan, K. (1969). *Microteaching.* Reading, Mass: Addison-Wesley.

Erickson, F. (1986). Qualitative methods in research on teaching. In M.C. Wittrock (Ed.), *Handbook of research on teaching*, (3rd ed.). New York: MacMillan Publishing Company, 119-161.

Flanders, N.A. (1970). *Analyzing teaching behavior.* Reading, Massachusetts: Addison-Wesley Publishing Company.

Hoover, K.H. (1980). *College teaching today: A handbook for postsecondary instruction.* Boston: Allyn and Bacon, Inc.

McKenna, B.H. (1981). Context/environment effects in teacher evaluation. In J. Millman (Ed.), *Handbook of teacher evaluation.* Beverly Hills, CA: Sage Publications.

Miles, M.B. & Huberman, A.M. (1984). *Qualitative data analysis: A sourcebook of new methods.* Beverly Hills, CA: Sage Publications.

Smith, R.A. & Swartz, F.S. (1985). A theory of effectiveness: Faculty development case studies. *To improve the academy. 4,* 63-74. Professional and Organizational Development Network in Higher Education.

Karron G. Lewis is a Faculty Development Specialist in the Center for Teaching Effectiveness. Her academic background is in Music Education and Educational Curriculum & Instruction with emphasis on the Observation and Analysis of Classroom Interactions. She welcomes comments and suggestions and can be reached at: Center for Teaching Effectiveness, Main Building 2200, The University of Texas at Austin, Austin, TX 78712-1111. (512) 471-1488.

Consultation Using a Research Perspective

Jody D. Nyquist
Donald H. Wulff
Center for Instructional Development & Research
University of Washington

Consultation processes used to assist instructors in making instructional changes in their courses can be approached in numerous ways. Although our earliest consulting attempts with faculty at the Center for Instructional Development and Research (CIDR) at the University of Washington were not based on a particular model or approach, we soon realized through trial and error experimentation that our most successful consultations emerged when we:

1. collected baseline data for instructors to be used for diagnosis and problem identification (a *data collection* step);

2. assisted instructors in analyzing the data (a *data analysis* step);

3. provided suggestions or recommendations based on the analysis of data from a specific course within a particular discipline (a *data interpretation* step); and

4. outlined with the instructor specific implementation strategies for modifying instructor behavior, classroom procedures, or course documentation (a *data translation* step).

Over and over we were struck with the similarity between the phases involved in faculty consultations in which the client seemed most pleased and the steps required by the various research studies with which we were concurrently involved. The traditional research steps of forming a problem, developing the methods of investigation, determining the results, and reporting the conclusions inferred from the results became the basis of our consultations.

In retrospect, the need and desirability for this kind of approach seem fairly obvious. Using an application of the traditional research process enables the instructional consultant to use a process familiar to professors to assist them to make significant instructional modifications in their classes without requiring new ways of thinking. Thus, the approach is both systematic and complete and also familiar and appealing to the client—the individual professor or graduate teaching assistant.

A Research Perspective

So what does it mean for the instructional consultant to assume a research perspective or to be a classroom researcher in someone else's classroom? In the first place, this perspective defines the role of the instructional developer or consultant in relation to the classroom instructor—the client. We see ourselves as classroom researchers gathering data that will be useful for the instructor to inform his or her decision-making. The classroom becomes a place where we gather data, where we research what goes on between students and instructors. This research perspective limits and describes our involvement. We are, then, data collectors and analyzers; we are not classroom evaluators. We are not counselors. We are responsible to our client, the individual classroom instructor, and no one else. Thus, this research perspective guides our relationships with instructors.

Secondly, this research perspective precludes our feeling that we must have answers. We become, instead, investigators in a partnership relationship with a particular instructor, attempting to find the answers to an individual's instructional questions. The approach eliminates the possibility of applying standardized, generic, predetermined suggestions or recommendations for unique, often idiosyncratic, contextual and discipline-specific teaching difficulties. This perspective also keeps us from moving directly from problems to solutions without a careful analysis of the complexities of the particular instructional situation.

Thirdly, the research perspective enables us to have great confidence in the data we use as the basis for collaborating with the instructor to develop strategies for change. Using established quantitative and qualitative research methodologies, we repeatedly test the accuracy and validity of the findings. These valid and reliable data, rather than personal, or even expert, opinion, dictate what ought to be done to assist the instructor.

A Model for Consultation

As previously indicated, our consultation model represents an adaptation of the traditional research steps. Those steps, 1) identification of the research question, 2) collection of data, 3) analysis of data, 4) interpretation of data, and 5) development of implications based on findings or recommendations for further studies (Kerlinger, 1986), provide the underlying structure. As reflected in **Figure 1**, our modification, for consultation purposes, relabels the steps as: 1) identification of problem, issue or question; 2) collection of data; 3) analysis of data; 4) interpretation of data; and, finally, 5) translation of data. The model as displayed requires movement through the five basic phases with possible return to any step as the process proceeds and reveals significant findings and/or insights into what is occurring.

Identification of Problem/Issue/Question

As with any research process, our first step is to identify the appropriate question. Typically, the questions emerge in the initial interview between the consultant and the instructor. Problems, issues, questions may range from concerns about a set of student ratings to concerns about how to restructure an entire course, or how to introduce writing or small group activities to how to adopt a new way of evaluating student performance. By the end of the initial interview, however, the consultant and the faculty member will have clearly in mind what kinds of questions the faculty member is trying to address.

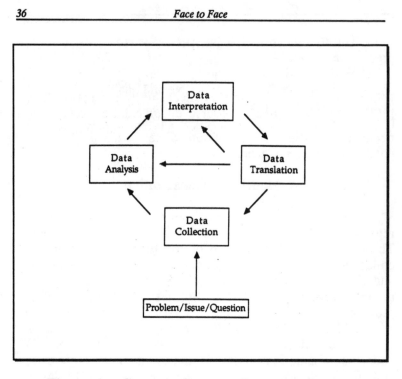

Figure 1. Consultation: A Research Process

Collection of Data

We then begin collecting data about a particular course and the instructor's interaction with students over that course material. We note or count everything we can think of in the classroom environment. We use quantitative research methods—class surveys, student ratings data, experimental designs complete with outside control groups—any method that will enable us to see what is going on with a particular group of students inside and outside the specific classroom setting. We use qualitative research methods including field observations, videotaping, student and faculty interviews, content analysis of class documents, collection of critical incidents. We are intrigued with any way of systematically collecting data whether it be student-teacher stories, anecdotes, perception measures, or quantitatively scaled evaluation measures. We attempt to triangulate our data by using multiple types of data, sources, times of the term, methods, or researchers. At a minimum we collect student perception data, professor perception data, course documentation data, and, when available, student achievement data. In addition, we may add peer evaluation data, video critique data, classroom observation data, student achievement on standardized tests data, and so forth. The challenge is to collect sufficient information to provide insights into what is occurring in a particular context.

Analysis of Data

The next step, as in all research, is to analyze the information that has been collected. We use a repertoire of standard analyses from computing simple correlations to developing qualitative matrices of the data. We conduct statistical analyses, or juxtaposition descriptive information looking for themes, patterns, consistencies, inconsistencies, and discrepancies in the data. Using standard validity and reliability tests, we check and recheck to confirm the accuracy, completeness, and significance of the data. The data are analyzed and re-analyzed until we are confident that we have a clear picture of what is happening in a particular course.

Interpretation of Data

Next, we attempt to help the classroom instructor make sense of the analysis of the data. We try to assist in the systematic, accurate attachment of meaning to the findings. Instructors who are often not involved in looking at educational research are typically quite responsive to and appreciative of our attempts to assist them in interpreting the data to determine what is going on in their classrooms. Always, we point out that the data belong to the instructors. What instructors decide to do as a result of studying the data is their decision to make. The question we are interested in pursuing remains, "After viewing or seeing the data collected in your classroom, what are your concerns?" The identification of the primary concerns provides the initial direction for possible changes.

Translation of Data

The final phase of our model is designed to assist instructors in translating their concerns into goals and strategies for change. Possible targeted changes may occur in terms of changes in curriculum, course structure, or instructional methods. Analysis of student perception data, for example, might highlight how students believe that they learn best in a particular course and could suggest changes to enhance learning possibilities. Analyses of peer observation information or document reviews give us insights into what other experts feel should be taught in a given course. We work as a confederate with the instructor translate the analysis of data into targeted changes which show promise for enabling students to achieve the instructor's goals for the course. Following the implementation of change, we often go back into the classroom to collect new data and begin the cycle once more.

The familiar traditional research steps, then, form the basis of our consulting model. Our adaptation of this process has relabeled the steps to identification of the problem, collection of data, analysis of data, interpretation of data, and translation of data, with an emphasis on the final step of translation. Using this model we can accommodate complexities of particular course content, level of students, expectations for student achievement, instructor presentation style, classroom methods, instructional materials. The steps provide a systematic process for achieving change. Perhaps our application of the model can best be illustrated by using one of our case studies involving a professor in Social Work.

A Case Study of Consulting Using a Research Perspective

The Issue/Problem

This professor was concerned about his teaching in a course consisting of first year graduate students. The graduate level required course, which met in two hour sessions twice a week, consisted primarily of experienced social workers who were returning to school to obtain administrative degrees. The instructor thought that he had planned the course carefully and that, initially, students were learning from the information he was imparting; but four weeks into the quarter, he began to feel uneasy about the course. He sensed underlying currents of animosity, and finally experienced some open hostility from the students. He, therefore, wanted to analyze what was happening in the course and sought the assistance of our faculty consultation services. Our first step in working with the instructor was to collect appropriate data from his course.

Data Collection

First and second data sources. The first two sources of data included the perceptions reported by the instructor during the initial interview and student ratings information from the previous year when the professor had taught the course for the first time. We collected data from a third source by conducting a class interview which provided perceptions of students currently enrolled in the class. Finally, to provide additional data for studying the instructor's concerns, one of our instructional consultants conducted a classroom observation as an outside observer.

The initial interview, which established the first data source, moved through a series of questions eliciting the instructor's perspectives covering the content of the course, the goals of the course, methods of imparting course content, and the exams and assignments. Additionally, the instructor discussed his perceptions of what was working in the class and what might be improved. He reported that he was committed to the theory he was presenting as necessary background for social workers who were interacting daily with their clients but that he felt he was spending an inordinate amount of time organizing the content and preparing lectures. In spite of all his efforts, he perceived that students were responding negatively. In addition to signs of boredom and outright resentment from students during his presentations, he also perceived that students were defensive when he returned assignments that had been evaluated and graded. Although he felt he was working very hard in the course, he was disappointed and frustrated by the negative student reactions that he perceived.

A review of the instructor's student ratings of the course as it had been taught the previous year provided a second source of information. The ratings had been completed using the university's standard student ratings forms which consist of a series of instructional items rated on a six-point scale as follows: 0 = very poor; 1 = poor; 2 = fair; 3 = good; 4 = very good; 5 = excellent. The ratings for all the items on the instructor's student evaluations were well below the university-wide means. The two items that ranked the very lowest were "use of class time" (x = 1.78) and "instructor's effectiveness in teaching the subject matter" (x = 2.22). Other items that were rated very low included "relevance and usefulness of course content" (x = 2.33), "amount students learned in the course" (x = 2.33), and "the course as a whole" (x = 2.33). Students' "confidence in instructor's knowledge" (x = 2.78) and "student interest level" (x = 2.62) were also quite low. Among the items with the highest ratings were "instructor's interest in students' learning" (x = 3.78) and "instructor's preparation for class" (x = 3.22). As previously described, on the basis of this feedback, the instructor had attempted to respond to these items in his teaching of the current course by being more selective in the content for the course and by organizing his lectures so he could present as much relevant information as possible during each class period. He was now dismayed that his extended efforts were seemingly having little effect.

Third data source. Needing to reconcile the differences between the instructor's perceived efforts to attend to these student evaluations and the apparent results, we selected a student perception interview process to further clarify students' concerns as a third source of data about the course. This service, called small group instructional diagnosis (SGID) (Clark & Bekey, 1979), is a process of using class interviews with groups of students. The SGID method is a systematic procedure for collecting data about student experiences in a given course including what is helping students to learn, what can be changed to improve learning, and how specific improvements can be made. The procedure, which takes approximately a half-hour of class time, requires that the instructional consultant work directly with students in the class, in the absence of the instructor, to obtain the data. On the given day the instructional consultant asks students in the class to form groups, select a chair and come to consensus on the answers to three questions:

1. What is helping you to learn the content in this course?
2. What could be improved to assist you in learning the course content?
3. How would you suggest improvements be made?

Following a ten-minute discussion, groups are asked to report their ideas to the entire class. The instructional consultant summarizes the groups' ideas on the board or overhead, clarifying until group members are satisfied that the consultant understands completely the information being reported.

Fourth data source. The fourth source of data consisted of an observation conducted by the instructional consultant. The instructor chose to have the instructional consultant observe the classroom interaction during the hour-and-a-half immediately preceding the class interview process. The instructor and consultant agreed that the observation would be used to provide a description about what was happening in the class with particular attention to evidence of perceived student dissatisfaction with the course. The data collected during this consultant observation were then analyzed along with the interview information from the instructor and students and previous student ratings to provide the instructor with a comprehensive description of what was occurring in the classroom.

During the data collection stage, then, the consultant systematically employed a research perspective to gather information from four main sources: 1) the instructor himself during the initial interview; 2) the student ratings of the course from students who had been enrolled the previous year; 3) the class interview process used with students currently enrolled in the course; and 4) the observation conducted by the consultant.

Data Analysis

Since the data collected for this particular case were based primarily on the interviews and observation, they were analyzed using three methods of qualitative data analysis. As a first step, the instructional consultant identified the important instructional categories within the data from each source. To do this, the consultant first reviewed the notes from the initial interview, which yielded four instructional dimensions that were important from the instructor's viewpoint: theoretical content, organization and preparation, lecture and short question-answer periods as primary instructional methods, and student dissatisfaction. The categories identified in the student ratings the previous year were related to the instructor's organization and preparation, instructor's interest in students' learning, content, use of class time, and amount learned in the course. Overall, these ratings from previous students suggested extreme dissatisfaction with the course. The categories that emerged from the information provided by current students during the class interview process also identified similar categories: theoretical content, organization and structure of the course, the lecture as the dominant instructional mode, and students' overall dissatisfaction with the way the course was progressing. Two additional categories that emerged from the data from current students were related to instructor credibility and student knowledge and experience. Finally, the description provided by the consultant's observation data revealed the importance of a theoretical body of content, organization and structure issues, lecture as the dominant instructional method, general student disengagement, and virtually no questions from the students about the content.

The second step in the data analysis was to search for themes within the data from each source. This process of thematization consists of looking at the interrelationships among categories. For example, a theme in the professor's interview data was that the theoretical content was so important that it needed to be carefully structured for students and given to them in the most expeditious way, in this case by lecturing. A theme from the ratings of previous students, however, challenged this approach. Although the students gave higher ratings for the professor's preparation and concern about students' learning, they perceived that he was not using class time well. Consequently, students' ratings of the amount they learned were low. One theme that emerged from the interrelationships of categories within the interview data from current students was that because of the emphasis on large amounts of theoretical material, content was not made relevant, either through the use of the professor's own expertise in the field or through the use of the students' experience. Finally, a theme that emerged from the consultant's descriptive categories was that students were not engaged in the primary instructional process, the use of lecture.

Once data from these four separate sources were categorized and thematized, the third step in the data analysis process for this consultation was to compare and contrast the major categories of data across the three sources. A matrix was especially useful in this stage of the process as it provided a visual representation of the information (see **Table 1**). Down the left side of the matrix the categories that emerged in the data were listed, that is, content, instructional methods, student dissatisfaction, and so forth. Across the top of the matrix, the sources of information were listed, such as, professor, ratings from previous students, perceptions of current students, observer/consultant. Viewing the major categories of the data simultaneously from the four perspectives helped to identify the important inconsistencies in the way the course was being perceived. For instance, while all four sources indicated that theoretical content was important, there were clear inconsistencies between the instructor and the students in their perceptions of the amount

TABLE 1: Sample Matrix for Analysis of Data Across Sources for Case Study of Social Work Professor

IMPORTANT INSTRUCTIONAL DIMENSIONS THAT EMERGED	SOURCES OF INFORMATION			
	Professor	Previous Student Ratings (Based on 6-point scale; 0=Very poor; 5=Excellent)	Current Students	Observer/Consultant
Content	Theoretical emphasis	Heavy theoretical emphasis, relevance/usefulness of course content was poor ($\bar{x}$=2.33)	Heavy theoretical emphasis, too much theory, "use of relevant examples helpful," but little use of own expertise or student experience	Theoretical emphasis
Organization/ preparation	Strong organization, structure and preparation	Instructor's preparation was good ($\bar{x}$=3.22)	Well prepared, organized for class	Clear, well organized
Instructional method(s)	Lecture to present important theoretical information; short question-answer periods, present as much relevant information as possible	Poor use of class time ($\bar{x}$=1.78)	Lecture as dominant mode, wasted valuable time, need for interaction with professor and other students, use student expertise, no opportunity for integration of content	Lecture as dominant mode, no questions from students, teacher-centered
Student attitude	Dissatisfaction, boredom, underlying animosity, open hostility, defensiveness	Low rating of the course as a whole ($\bar{x}$=2.33), low student interest level ($\bar{x}$=2.62)	Extreme dissatisfaction, hostility, resentment	Disengagement, no participation
Instructor credibility	——	Poor-fair confidence in instructor's knowledge ($\bar{x}$=2.78)	Low credibility because of use of inappropriate instructional methods, lack of expertise	——
Student knowledge/ experience	Experienced graduate students returning for administrative degrees, lacking knowledge of administration	Primarily experienced social workers	Experienced social work knowledge/expertise was not being	Mature learners
Amount learned in course	Students "seem to be learning"	Low ($\bar{x}$=2.33)	Dissatisfied with amount learned, credibility in assessing learning	——
Instructor effectiveness	"Planned the course carefully," "attempted to respond to previous feedback"	"Interested" in students' learning ($\bar{x}$=3.78), low ratings of instructor's effectiveness ($\bar{x}$=2.22)	Ineffective because of lack of credibility and inappropriate instructional methods	Genuine instructor concern, one-way communication

of theoretical content that should be included and of the ways that the content could be integrated into students' practice of social work administration. This data analysis across sources also revealed that even though the course content was well-organized and potentially important, there were discrepancies between the ways in which the instructor and the students thought the content might best be imparted. While the instructor felt that lecture was the best way to impart such important information, students wanted to interact more fully with the instructor and other students so they could integrate the information into their own experiences and assess it in terms of their own expertise. In addition, while the instructor believed that theories provided the content of the course, students, on the other hand, perceived that their own experience and expertise and the field experience of the instructor could make significant contributions to the course content. Because the instructor did not make use of his own field experience, students began to suspect that he had little administrative experience; and consequently, attacked his credibility. Furthermore, because of this lack of credibility, students felt that the instructor was unable to assess the extent to which they could integrate such theoretical content into their own extensive experience; thus, they resented the instructor's attempts to grade their assignments. These inconsistencies, particularly between the perceptions of the instructor and the students, provided the basis for much of the instructor-student dissatisfaction with the class. The classroom observation by the consultant was particularly useful for revealing how the inconsistencies actually manifested themselves in the classroom.

Data Interpretation

The process of interpreting the data consisted primarily of the consultant's helping the instructor to make sense of the information. Although it is impossible to discuss this process in detail, we thought it useful to highlight two models or theories that the consultant employed in interpreting the data.

In this particular case, prior to the meeting with the professor, the consultant thought about ways to interpret the results. The consultant selected a model of instruction (Kibler, Cegala, Watson, Barker, & Miles, 1981) which identifies the phases of the instructional process in which difficulties might occur: setting goals and objectives, conducting preassessment, selecting instructional procedures, and evaluating instruction (see **Figure 2**). Typically, such models function as lenses primarily to assist the consultant in deriving insights about the data; and although the models may be briefly described or may provide structure for the interpretation of data with the instructor, the consultant is careful to focus on the interpretation of data rather than the examination of the use of models.

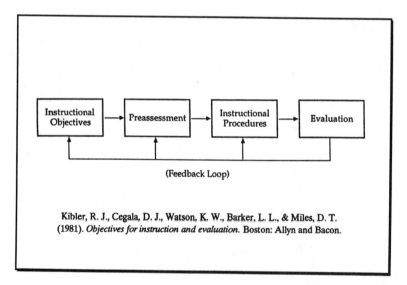

Kibler, R. J., Cegala, D. J., Watson, K. W., Barker, L. L., & Miles, D. T. (1981). *Objectives for instruction and evaluation.* Boston: Allyn and Bacon.

Figure 2. A General Model of Instruction

The data interpretation process continued when the consultant met with the professor. Since rapport and trust had previously been established, the consultant reviewed the data collection and analysis processes that had been completed and highlighted important categories and themes that had emerged from the data. The consultant's analysis, using the Kibler et al. (1981) model, had identified the preassessment phase as an area to pursue with the professor. Immediately the discussion began to focus on the ways this group of students might be different from traditional undergraduate students. The discussion subsequently led to the use of information from adult learning theory, the second theory or framework to be employed in the interpretation of the data.

The consultant pointed out that emerging theories of adult learning (Knowles, 1978) suggest the importance of using the experience of adult learners as a resource to be incorporated in the classroom, particularly since adults typically return to school with a strong problem-solving orientation that will allow them to address very specific needs. The instructor very soon began to make sense of the data in terms of such adult learning theory. It became clear, for instance, that if the students had extensive social work experience, they might want to use that experience to analyze the theories presented in class and to integrate the content in terms of their own needs. Such an instructional goal on the part of the learners would require appropriate instructional strategies. Since lecture as the primary strategy in the course was not allowing these adult learners to interact in ways that would allow them to apply, analyze, synthesize, and evaluate the theories in terms of their own experiences, the students were soon frustrated and dissatisfied. In addition, from their perceptions, a professor who could not recognize the importance of the students' experience in such a course lacked credibility and should not be evaluating them.

Using results of the data analysis and the basic instructional and adult learning models and theories, then, the consultant continued to work with the instructor to interpret the results. The students in the social work class were feeling disenchanted with a class in which large amounts of information were imparted primarily through the use of the lecture method without using the experience of the learners. These insights were helpful in answering the original questions about what was going on in the class that was resulting in such resentful behaviors from the students in the class.

Data Translation

Translating the data was a process of moving the instructor from the meaning of the data to the stage of developing strategies to improve instruction in the course. Once the consultant and the instructor had discussed various interpretations of the data, the consultant asked the instructor to identify the areas in the feedback that concerned him most. The instructor was concerned that students could not see the value of all the theories but recognized the importance of trying to use the experience of the adult learners. He was concerned that all his preparation and planning was not having much impact on students' overall rating of the course or on the instructor's contribution to the course.

Once the instructor identified the major areas of his concern in the feedback, the consultant assisted him in setting specific goals for change. The instructor chose the following goals:

1. to decrease the number of theories addressed in the remaining portion of the course,

2. to increase the amount of student-to-student and student-to-teacher interaction that would make use of both instructor and student expertise and knowledge in the class, and

3. to create assignments that would require that students apply the theories to their own specific experiences in the field.

Once goals were set, the next step was to develop specific strategies for achieving the goals. The professor and consultant focused primarily on ways, especially the use of teacher-led discussion, for increasing classroom interaction, and began to design assignments in small groups.

Finally, follow-up occurred. Since the instructor chose to alter the primary instructional method of lecture, he wanted additional assistance with leading discussion. So, he and the consultant met subsequently to design a teacher led discussion over the theoretical content and to determine how additional feedback about his success with that process might be gathered.

The instructor chose to have the consultant visit the class again to observe a teacher led discussion and provide feedback about the kinds of questions asked and the overall level of student enthusiasm and participation.

Conclusion

The case study, then, demonstrates the use of a research perspective in our consulting work. The perspective defines our instructional consultant role and lets the individual instructor own the process. Ultimately the instructor makes the decisions about the research questions, about the ways to gather data, about instructional changes that should be implemented and about the ways the changes will be implemented. In addition, because the process is data based, the issue of the consultant as an evaluator of teaching is eliminated. Rather, we work side by side with the instructor as a researcher, a resource, and a confidant. Furthermore, taking a research perspective helps us recognize that the stages of data interpretation and translation often raise additional questions. We may not have all the answers. But good research generates good questions and produces the possibility for follow-up and further investigation which requires collection, analysis, interpretation, and translation of additional data.

As we continue to work with the model, we expect to modify our application of it and to develop further insights derived from our use of it. At present, however, our conceptualization of consultation using a research perspective has enabled us to recognize the complexity of the consultation process, a process with which instructors are already familiar. We offer this consultation model as an approach which may be of value for use with instructors on your campus.

References

Clark, J. & Bekey, J. (1979). Use of small groups in instructional evaluation. *POD Quarterly, 1,* 87-95.

Kerlinger, F.N. (1986). *Foundations of behavioral research* (3rd ed.). New York: Holt, Rinehart and Winston.

Kibler, R.J., Cegala, D.J., Watson, K.W., Barker, L.L., & Miles, D.T. (1981). *Objectives for instruction and evaluation* (2nd ed.). Boston: Allyn and Bacon.

Knowles, M. (1978). *The adult learner: A neglected species.* Houston, TX: Gulf Publishing Co.

Jody D. Nyquist is the Director for Instructional Development at the Center for Instructional Development and Research at the University of Washington in Seattle. Her academic background is in Speech Communication and she has been engaged in faculty development related activities since 1973.

Donald H. Wulff in an Instructional Development Specialist at the Center for Instructional Development and Research at the University of Washington in Seattle. His academic background is in Interpersonal and Instructional Communication and he has been engaged in faculty development related activities since 1980. They welcome comments and suggestions and can be reached at: Center for Instructional Development and Research, University of Washington, 107 Parrington, DC-07, Seattle, WA 98195 , (206) 543-6588.

Using Qualitative Methods to Generate Data for Instructional Development

Jody D. Nyquist
Donald H. Wulff
Center for Instructional Development and Research
University of Washington

Instructional and faculty development consultants are continually searching for ways to assist instructors in solving their instructional problems. As Smith and Schwartz (1985) suggest, faculty consultants must first elicit valid information which can be used to provide instructors with insights about the quality of their teaching. This information is then used to identify any problems the instructor may have and to provide baseline data against which instructional improvement can be measured. Inherent within that information, also, are the recommendations and suggestions for instructional development. In typical faculty development consultations, data are collected, analyzed, and translated into instructor behavior goals in a process which should be followed by adaptation of instruction and further evaluation.

This process essentially requires a research approach with systematic data collection, data analysis and interpretation of findings. As with any problem-solving effort, the entire process must be based on verifiable, valid and reliable data. The contention in this paper, therefore, is that: 1) data collected to assist instructors in improving their teaching effectiveness must meet certain criteria and 2) qualitative research methods provide useful ways of generating such data.

*This chapter is adapted from an earlier article: Wulff, Donald H. and Nyquist, Jody D. (1986). Using qualitative methods to generate data for instructional development. *To improve the academy, 5,* 37-46. The Professional and Organizational Development Network in Higher Education and The National Council for Staff, Program and Organizational Development.

Data Requirements for Instructional Development

In order to be optimally useful, data collected for the improvement of instruction need to be a certain kind. Collecting such data is particularly difficult in teaching contexts for several reasons:

1. teaching environments are extremely complex;

2. effective teachers represent a wide range of idiosyncratic behaviors and styles;

3. the roles of students and student-teacher relationships vary from context to context; and

4. different courses require differences in course goals, daily objectives, and student outcomes.

Given these variables, data useful for instructional development must meet the following criteria:

1. the data must represent the complexity of classroom environments.

2. the data must include context variables.

3. the data must incorporate the perspectives of classroom participants whether they be teachers, students, visitors, and/or administrators.

4. the data must represent the specific case.

The goal of collecting this kind of data is to describe in a clear and substantial form what is going on in a dynamic, extremely complex, instructor and discipline-specific environment. From that description, then, the researcher can extract instructor behaviors and curricular frameworks which inhibit or enable students to learn the material being covered.

As previously explained, great care must be taken to ensure that these descriptions are based on data that meet the four criteria. The data must represent the complexity of the classroom environment, include contextual variables, incorporate the perspectives of classroom participants, and represent the specific case. We have found that qualitative research methods provide an effective way of collecting such data.

Qualitative Methods for Instructional Development

Defining Qualitative Methods

Philipsen (1982), in his discussion of the qualitative case study, suggests that qualitative inquiry is *in situ,* exploratory, openly-coded, and participatory. He explains these dimensions of qualitative inquiry in the following way:

> The investigator searches the contexts in which the phenomena of interest occur naturally without deliberately producing the phenomena; explores the phenomena of interest by describing it without total reliance upon pre-determined codes or categories; and uses his or her own experiencing of the phenomena as one source of insight into it. (p.10)

This explanation is useful for suggesting what qualitative inquiry entails.

Patton's (1980) discussion of what qualitative data look like explains the kind of information that can be obtained from an inquiry process such as the one Philipsen (1982) described. According to Patton (1980), the kind of information collected from a qualitative measurement process includes detailed descriptions, direct quotations, and excerpts or passages from written documents (p.22). The primary methods of collecting qualitative data are interviewing, observing, and studying documents. Data collected by these means tend to be useful for instructional development.[1]

---

[1]For a thorough and relatively straightforward description of "how to" collect qualitative data in the various forms of interview, observation, and document study, see Goetz & LeCompte (1984), Lincoln & Guba (1985), or Patton (1980).

Employing Qualitative Methods for Collecting Useful Data

Classroom complexity. Qualitative methods meet the first criterion for useful data by providing a way to capture the interactive complexity of the classroom environment. Numerous researchers contend that although traditional research approaches have been insightful in many ways, they should not be relied on as the only sources of data with which to study teaching effectiveness. Pedersen (1975) observes that the teaching-learning sequence contains variables that are so numerous and complex in their interaction with one another that the process is difficult to define and study: "The teacher's influence upon educational outcomes interacts with the influence of so many other agents that it becomes extremely difficult to determine with much certainty the effects of a particular teacher upon a particular pupil" (p. 13). The exploratory nature of qualitative methods, however, provides a way for the variables to emerge without the constraints of predetermined units and measurement categories. As Cooper (1982) suggests:

> Classroom teaching is indeed complex and interactive. To get inside the instructional process, inquiry methods are needed which allow the consultant and instructor to examine parts while not losing sight of the whole; to explore the event from within while standing outside and looking in; to fix an event in time while remembering that in its context it is ongoing; to attend to various views of the same event; and to remain flexible and open to ideas. The fieldwork techniques of school ethnographies provide means to examine, analyze, and understand the interaction dynamics and the structure of classroom teaching. (p. 2)

Context. Qualitative methods meet the second criterion for useful data by providing a way to incorporate context variables in the study of the teaching-learning process. Although the importance of the context in research on teaching has clearly been advocated by many educators, the importance of considering the context in specific efforts to improve teaching was most directly stressed by McKenna (1981):

> Success in teaching, however, defined and assessed, is highly contextual. Therefore, if evaluation of teaching and teachers is to serve meaningful and useful purposes, it must not only identify and

define all the mitigating contexts but must also take into account their influences, both constructive and negative, in determining success. (p. 23)

Participant perspectives. Qualitative methods meet the third criterion for useful data by allowing for the incorporation of the perspectives of the participants. According to Wilson (1977), the qualitative perspective assumes that people are knowing beings whose behavior must be considered as purposive. It does not assume, however, that "similar expressions of behavior by different people necessarily have similar meanings" (Bussis, Chittenden, & Amarel, 1976, p.14). Erickson (1986) is among the most recent to suggest the importance of the *local meanings* that happenings have for the people involved in them: "In different classrooms, schools, and communities, events that seem ostensibly the same may have distinctly differing local meanings." (p. 212). Although the importance of understanding the perspectives of the participants in the teaching-learning context has been articulated by numerous researchers (Bussis, Chittenden, & Amarel, 1976; Fenstermacher, 1979; Staton-Spicer, 1982; Wilson, 1977), the importance of qualitative methods as a way of understanding those perspectives was most directly articulated by Cooper (1981):

A naturalistic research process which employs multiple methods and taps the conscious and tacit knowledge of the instructor, students, and researcher enables us to describe *how* the dynamics of the instructional process are produced and interpreted . . . . The more that is known about what behaviors mean, the closer we can come to behaving in ways to accomplish the results desired. (p. 36)

Specific case. Finally, qualitative methods meet the fourth criterion for useful data by allowing the instructional improvement process to focus on specifics. As Erickson (1986), suggests:

Answering the question, "What is happening?" with a general answer often is not very useful. "The teacher (or students) in this classroom is (are) on task" often doesn't tell us the specific details that are needed in order to understand the points of view of the actors involved. (p. 121)

Fieldwork methods, however, have the potential for providing specific understanding "through documentation of concrete details of practice" (Erickson, 1986, p. 121).

Typical Applications for Instructional Development

One way of increasing understanding of the use of qualitative methods for instructional development is simply to discuss specific cases. The following cases, then, are presented as specific applications of qualitative methods to gather information for instructor and course improvement.

Case #1

An instructor teaching a course in the sciences was concerned about how his course was progressing. He was particularly concerned because he had taught the course once before, and the student ratings of the course on that occasion were well below the average for the University. Although he had used the original feedback to implement changes in the instructional dimensions concerned with organization, rapport, relevance of content, and interaction in the classroom, he was concerned about the usefulness of those changes for improving the course for this new group of students. As a result of his consultation with a faculty development specialist, this instructor's present concerns suggested need for the following:

1. Immediate feedback about the present course;

2. Assessment of teaching data sources in addition to student opinion;

3. Sufficient detail about organization, rapport, content, relevance and interaction to assist in evaluating changes that had been implemented;

4. Open-ended measurement that would allow for the emergence of variables specific to the way the class is presently being taught;

5. A process with minimal infringement on class time and the time of the instructor.

Based on these needs, the instructor and consultant selected consultant observation and interviews with instructor and students as qualitative methods for gathering data. Observational data were gathered during a two-hour classroom visitation during the fourth week of the term. Interview data were gathered from the instructor during the consultation with the consultant and during in-class interviews conducted with students during the fifth week of the term. Information for this faculty member, then, was collected from instructor, the students and the observer.

The instructor's perception data were gathered during an interview with the consultant. Although the major purpose of that interview was to establish goals and procedures for the faculty development process, the interview also provided insights about the instructional variables that the instructor considered most important. During the interview the instructor discussed course content, instructional goals and strategies, his perceptions of the quality of instruction in the course, and appropriate strategies for obtaining information about the course. From this information the following variables were identified by the instructor as important in this particular instructional process: content, organization, rapport, relevance, and interaction.

The second source of information for collecting data about the course was the interview conducted with the students. Because of the time limitations, data were obtained through a process called small-group instructional diagnosis (SGID) which allows the students to be interviewed collectively (Clark & Bekey, 1979). The process requires a facilitator who can meet with the students, in the absence of the instructor, to obtain information about the course. On the given day, the facilitator instructs students in the class to form small groups, select a chair and come to consensus on three questions: 1) What do you like about the course? 2) What do you think needs improvement? 3) How would you suggest improvements be made? Following a ten-minute discussion period, the groups report their deliberations to the class while the facilitator summarizes the groups' ideas, clarifying until group members are satisfied that the consultant understands the information being reported. Analysis of these data revealed that students perceived the major problems in the class to be related to content, time management, expectations, relevance, instructor confidence/autocracy, consistency in use of labels, and evaluation.

A third data base for this case consisted of observational information obtained by the consultant who attended the class. Using the variables identified by the instructor in the initial interview, the consultant entered the classroom with the general question, "What is the quality of instruction in this class?" Although the variables provided a sensitizing framework to alert the researcher to certain categories of the instruction, they were not intended to preclude the emergence of other variables that the observer considered significant in the instruction in the class. From this data source, the major instructional variables which emerged tended to be related to content, organization, student questions, student-to-student interaction, rapport, instructor confidence, and relevance.

Three data sources based on the perceptions of the instructor, the students, and the observer provided information with which to study the instructional problem in this case. Although time constraints precluded development of the thick description commonly associated with qualitative inquiry, the use of three different perspectives allowed for comparison of the major instructional categories that emerged. This comparison provided understanding of variables that most readily needed to be addressed by the instructor. The opportunity to observe in the classroom and to probe specific perceptions during the interviews provided concrete information which the consultant and professor could use to set goals for modifying the course. Thus, the data collected through the qualitative methods of observation and interview were analyzed and translated into target goals for instructional change.[2]

---

[2] Researchers using qualitative methods need to become familiar with specific analytic procedures including the use of conceptual frameworks and matrices. For discussion of qualitative data analysis, see Goetz & LeCompte (1984), Miles and Huberman (1984), and Patton (1980).

Case #2

A second case study represents the application of qualitative research methods for a course which was viewed as a departmental problem. The contact was initiated by the department chair in a professional program. The required course, which met all day long, one day a week, contained both a lecture and a laboratory component. In the mornings the fifty students attended two-hour lectures delivered by the same professor for the entire term. The remaining seven hours of each day were spent in the laboratory where students worked individually under the supervision of one of seven lab instructors.

An initial interview with the department chair suggested that the primary concern was the amount of time it was taking students to complete projects in the laboratory portion of the class. The chair reported that the lab instructors suspected that students were having difficulty transferring their learning from the lecture to the laboratory. Consequently, he was interested in specific instructional strategies which would assist students in applying the lecture material in the laboratory. He perceived, however, that students procrastinated, failed to use the laboratory manual, and expected to finish projects outside regularly scheduled laboratory time. As a result, they were not taking advantage of the supervision available during regularly scheduled laboratory hours. In addition, he felt that the existence of an "attitude problem" might be affecting students' ability to finish projects on time. He was interested in a student input that would assist the lab instructors in improving the course and eliminating the problems. As a result of the initial interview with the department chair, the following information needs were established:

1. an open-ended way of obtaining information to confirm or disconfirm the chair's perceptions;

2. a process detailed enough to provide concrete information for the improvement of the course.

Because of the need for an open-ended approach that provided a detailed description of what was happening in the course, it was decided to use the qualitative methods of observation and interview to obtain data for the case. The interview data were obtained from the department chair and the students. The observational data were compiled by the consultants who worked on the project. The primary sources of data for this case, then, were the department chair, the observers and the students.

The chair provided qualitative input in two ways. First he provided information in the initial interview with the consultants. At that time he discussed his concerns about the course and his perceptions of the reasons for the course difficulties. After the initial interview, he was asked to write responses to open-ended questions about goals of the course, instructors' expectations, and the relationship between the lecture and laboratory components of the course. From these data bases, it was determined that the variables of major concern to the director were related to use of laboratory time, completion deadlines, the link between the lecture and the laboratory, use of instructors' expertise during laboratory time, instructional strategies to increase student efficiency, and student attitudes that might be affecting the course.

Two consultants observed in the lecture and laboratory components of the course to develop perspectives on the most important instructional variables to be considered. The observers attended both the lecture and the laboratory sections of the course for ten collective hours. They used the variables identified by the director as a framework to sensitize them to possible areas of difficulty. However, they remained open to the emergence of variables that had not been previously identified by the department chair. From the observational data, the major instructional variable that needed to be addressed was related to expectations for the course. Analysis of observational data suggested that it would be important to clarify expectations about the course and the roles of the lecture, the laboratory, the instructors, and the students in meeting those expectations. These major areas of need, then, were used to develop the schedule of questions for interviews with the students.

Interviews with students provided the third, and primary, source of information for assessing the course. Using questions that focused students on expectations for the course and ways to meet those expectations, the consultants conducted one-to-one interviews with 37 of the students in the class (74% of the population). Each interview lasted 15-20 minutes. These interviews then provided not only major areas of student concern but also specific suggestions about how the course might be improved. Major areas of concern identified by the students were related to the link between lecture and laboratory, evaluation procedures in lecture and laboratory, amount of time spent working outside the laboratory, instructional strategies in the laboratory, and class atmosphere and reinforcement. The interview data provided detailed descriptions and quotations with which to clarify students' perceptions and make specific recommendations for improving the course.

Results of this study were then carefully processed to determine the most significant variables to be considered in setting goals for improvement. Because of the use of several different perspectives, it was possible to compare the information across data sources. This process allowed the consultants to determine that there were inconsistencies in the students' and instructors' perceptions of the course. With the detailed information from the interviews, the consultants were able to identify not only major areas of change for the course but also specific ways in which those changes might be implemented. This approach resulted in a set of recommendations which were quickly adopted and implemented by the department.

Summary

The basic contention of this chapter is that data collected to assist instructors in improving their teaching effectiveness must meet certain criteria and that qualitative research methods provide useful ways of generating such data. In both these case studies, the information collected met the four criteria for useful data. The data represented the complexity of the classroom environments, included context variables, incorporated the perspectives of the participants, and described the specific cases. Qualitative methods provided a way, then, of collecting information that could be analyzed, interpreted and translated into recommendations and changes for both courses.

Ideally, all instructors would be willing to spend enough time on their teaching to use a variety of qualitative methods in their efforts. Such efforts, then could incorporate observation in the natural environment, videotape, interviews, and study of documents as qualitative methods useful for collecting data to improve teaching. Ongoing teacher improvement efforts using this greater variety of strategies would be taking advantage of the full potential of qualitative methods. Realistically, however, many instructors are limited by the amount of time they can and will contribute to improved teaching efforts. As a result, the specific applications in this chapter are typical examples of what can be accomplished using qualitative methods to meet the needs of busy instructors. It is hoped that faculty development consultants can use ideas from this chapter as an impetus to creatively about the variety of ways that qualitative methodology can be employed to generate data useful for improving teaching effectiveness.

References

Bussis, A., Chittended, E.A., & Amarel, M. (1976). *Beyond surface curriculum: An interview study of teacher's uderstandings.* Boulder, CO: Westview Press.

Clark, J. and Bekey, J. (1979). Use of small groups in instructional evaluation. *POD Quarterly. 1,* 87-95.

Cooper, C.R. (1981). Different ways of being a teacher: An ethnographic study of a college instructor's academic and social roles in the classroom. *Journal of Classroom Interaction, 16,* 27-37.

Cooper, C.R. (1982). Getting inside the instruction process. *Journal of Instructional Development, 5,* 2-10.

Erickson, F. (1986). Qualitative methods in research on teaching. In M. C. Wittrock (Ed.), *Handbook of research on teaching* (Third ed.). New York: MacMillan Publishing Company, 119-161.

Fenstermacher, G.D. (1979). A philosophical consideration of recent research on teacher effectiveness. In L.S. Shulman (Ed.), *Review of Research in Education, 6.* Itasca, IL: Peacock, 157-185.

Goetz, J.P. & LeCompte, M.D. (1984). *Ethnography and qualitative design in educational research*. Orlando: Academic Press, Inc.

Lincoln, Y.S. & Guba, E.G. (1985). *Naturalistic inquiry*. Beverly Hills, CA: Sage Publications.

McKenna, B.H. (1981). Context/environment effects in teacher evaluation. In J. Millman (ed.), *Handbook of teacher evaluation*. Beverly Hills, CA: Sage Publications.

Miles, M.B. & Huberman, A.M. (1984). *Qualitative data analysis: A sourcebook of new methods*. Beverly Hills, CA: Sage Publications.

Patton, M.Q. (1980). *Qualitative evaluation methods*. Beverly Hills, CA: Sage Publications.

Pedersen, K.G. (1975). Improving teacher effectiveness. *Education Canada, 15*, 13-20.

Philipsen, G. (1982). The qualitative case study as a strategy in communication inquiry. *The Communicator, 12*, 4-17.

Smith, R.A. & Swartz, F.S. (1985). A theory of effectiveness: Faculty development case studies. *To improve the academy*. Professional and Organizational Development Network in Higher Education, 63-74.

Staton-Spicer, A.Q. (1982). Qualitative inquiry in instructional communication: Applications and directions. *The Communicator, 12*, 35-46.

Wilson, S. (1977). The use of ethnographic techniques in educational research. *Review of Educational Research, 47*, 245-265.

Jody D. Nyquist is the Director for Instructional Development at the Center for Instructional Development and Research at the University of Washington in Seattle. Her academic background is in Speech Communication and she has been engaged in faculty development related activities since 1973.

Donald H. Wulff in an Instructional Development Specialist at the Center for Instructional Development and Research at the University of Washington in Seattle. His academic background is in Interpersonal and Instructional Communication and he has been engaged in faculty development related activities since 1980. They welcome comments and suggestions and can be reached at: Center for Instructional Development and Research, University of Washington, 107 Parrington, DC-07, Seattle, WA 98195 , (206) 543-6588.

Part II:
Some Specific Methods of Consultation for Instructional Improvement

In this section the authors explore a variety of methods and techniques which they employ in their individual consultation programs. These techniques work well for each of these people and all of them have realized teaching improvement in their clients while using them. You are encouraged to use these descriptions as a spring-board for starting your own program or as a catalyst for making changes in a program which you have been using for awhile.

The periodic workshop has been a mainstay in faculty development programs almost since the beginning. In this discussion, Mary Pat Mann gives pointers for using these workshops as a way to encourage faculty members to take part in individual consultation.

Joyce Povlacs describes the format of the Teaching Analysis Process, the program of individual consultation in use at the University of Nebraska-Lincoln. She emphasizes that the model may be varied to suit the situation and gives the roles the consultant must play in the process. The case Povlacs recounts demonstrates one instructor's reliance on the questionnaire Teaching Analysis By Students (TABS) to improve his teaching.

At St. Olaf College, Barbara Helling has trained undergraduate students to act as in-class observers and feedback agents for faculty members. The students are trained in observation skills and attend every class session. They assist faculty members in recognizing incongruencies between the objectives stated by the instructor and what is actually happening.

Another way to provide student feedback to an instructor is described by Tiberius in the next chapter. By interviewing a random sample of the students in a class, the consultant can gain many insights into what is perceived by the students as effective and what is not. This information can then be shared with the faculty member and strategies for change or modification can be discussed.

The last two chapters in this section describe information-gathering techniques which are somewhat more objective. First, Karron Lewis discusses an objective observation system, based on Flander's Interaction Analysis, which can be used to provide very detailed feedback about instructor-student interactions in a classroom. Then, David Taylor-Way utilizes the wonder of camcorders and videotape to stimulate faculty analysis of the motives behind their methods.

Individual Consultation and the Workshop: What's the Connection?

Mary Pat Mann
Coordinator of Faculty Development
Ohio University College of Osteopathic Medicine

Workshops have a bad name among some instructional consultants, particularly in ongoing development programs. They're seen as one-shot, short-term interventions that are not effective in promoting lasting change. But workshops can play an important role in establishing an individual consultation program, particularly when the consultant or the program is new. This article presents an alternative view of the traditional workshop, with suggestions for developing workshop programs that support individual consulting efforts.

Why Give a Workshop?

Traditionally, workshops focus on specific skills. Over the years, I've presented workshops like "How to Write Behavioral Objectives," "How to Prepare Overhead Transparencies," and "How to Write Good Test Items." The view was that workshops had to be pragmatic, giving participants something they could use in the classroom.

As time went on, such workshops fell into disfavor. Faculty most in need of new skills didn't come, it was hard to find new topics for the faithful who did come, and there was little evidence that the time and effort led to significant changes in behavior. Many developers turned to individual consultation and long-term interventions as more productive means to achieve program goals.

Individual consultation *can* be effective. But it is also costly, time-consuming, and invisible to all but those directly involved. So, in many development programs, the workshop lingers on. It remains as a low-cost way to reach faculty and a high-profile reminder of the existence of faculty development programs.

When I joined the Ohio University of Osteopathic Medicine, I faced the daunting prospect of coming up with interesting topics for the monthly workshop program. Soon, a larger problem led me to re-think the role of the workshop. How could I interest faculty in working with me on individual consultations? I was new, no one knew much about my skills or interests, and there hadn't been enough staff in the past to offer much individual consulting (that's why they added me...).

A second challenge also shaped my approach: Some faculty rejected opportunities to work with educational consultants because they felt pushed to adopt methods they disliked, or saw "educationists" as dogmatic and inflexible. How could I show faculty that consultation need not mean indoctrination and that differences of opinion were the rule rather than the exception in pedagogical circles?

As I began working with faculty, a third idea emerged: Faculty did not seem to realize that differences in teaching methods among colleagues reflected different values and attitudes, not bad habits. In discussing new projects with faculty, they often expressed the view that if everyone understood what was going on, they would all use Method X (or Y, or Z). How could I provide a forum for interaction that would allow faculty to discover this diversity?

These three factors developed into the workshop program:

1. to introduce faculty to ideas for consulting projects and to individual consultants;

2. to disseminate divergent ideas about teaching, thereby countering the image of educational consultants as inflexible; and

3. to provide opportunities for faculty to discuss their ideas and methods with each other.

The following sections describe the key components involved in implementing these goals, with examples drawn from actual workshops.

Goal 1:   Workshops as Exposure

Be organized. This is old hat, but becomes particularly important for the "new consultant in town." After all, how can you expect others to take your advice if you don't have your own act together? Workshop organization runs the gamut from behind-the-scenes preparation of the setting to sharpening your best group facilitation skills. Here are some pointers:

- *Set up dates, times, and topics as far in advance as possible.* Avoid last-minute changes. Changes will confuse your audience and disrupt their schedules; attendance will suffer.

- *Make sure the room is set up ahead of time —* don't ask participants to rearrange tables and chairs. Reserve the room at least one half hour ahead of your session. An early reservation gives you time to set up and will help prevent other meetings from running over time and forcing you to start late. Set up the food area ahead of time — particularly if you (like me) want to avoid the "hostess" image.

- *Provide refreshments if possible.* Our monthly workshops include lunch. We are not allowed to provide lunch for faculty and staff from regular university operating funds. Instead, a discretionary fund is used. Many colleges and universities have such special funds, although the rules for allocating them will differ.

  I am allowed to use discretionary funds partly because I don't use too much. We don't provide lavish meals, just enough to make it easy for faculty and staff to attend. Typical menus include meat and cheese trays for sandwiches, soup and salad, pizza, and Chinese food. The food comes from local restaurants and on-campus catering

services. Most places will deliver and will bill the
institution rather than asking for payment up front. We
keep our own supply of paper napkins, plates, and cups;
and also purchase our own juice and soft drinks to help
control costs.

Costs run about $3-$5 per person — Chinese food is the
cheapest. To keep costs down, you need accurate estimates
of how many will attend. I ask for RSVPs, but as the
workshops became established, people began coming
without notice — usually "regulars" and last-minute drop-
ins. I've become better at estimating numbers as I got to
know the audience better.

I don't really believe people attend just to eat, but it
makes a good excuse for those who need a rationalization
— and they attend!

- *Prepare an agenda*, but don't try to cover too much. An
over-stuffed agenda leads to lectures rather than discussion.
Plan workshops in sections, so that you can drop a section
if a good discussion gets started or add one if there are no
questions. If there are certain points you want the audience
to remember, prepare a handout. I generally provide
handouts of any overheads I present.

- *Be "up" for the workshop.* I'm nervous in front of groups,
so I use group facilitation techniques to prepare: Review
your agenda and try to anticipate responses to the points
you will bring up. What questions are likely to arise? Who
might agree or disagree? How should you respond? What
is the worst possible thing that could happen? (Usually, it's
that no one will have anything to say.) How can you deal
with it?

Be approachable. Your presentation style should be
consistent with your consulting style. I favor a process
consultation approach and try to reflect that in workshops.
This style means avoiding the "expert giving advice" method
of workshop presentations. Instead, this approach emphasizes
recognizing and building on skills faculty already have,

ensuring that projects meet faculty goals, and establishing a cooperative relationship.

This can be modeled in workshop settings by encouraging discussion instead of lecturing, calling on faculty in the audience to provide personal examples to illustrate specific points, and recognizing differences of opinion instead of pushing for consensus.

For example, the writing skills of medical students (or the lack thereof) often arose in discussions of testing methods. Attempts to use essay exams or papers were hampered by student problems with basic grammar. Should instructors take off points for spelling errors? Should we be teaching English in medical school?

A review of the literature revealed little on this topic, so I organized this workshop as a large-group discussion and served as the facilitator for the group. I began by asking faculty to share their experiences in giving writing assignments and their impressions of the writing skills of our students. When discussion lagged, I repeated faculty comments and asked other faculty to respond. We discovered two primary views on this topic among the faculty.

One group felt that medical school was no place for basic skills training in writing beyond what was needed to write adequate case notes. This group also emphasized the technical aspects of physician training, seeing the primary goal of the school as the production of skilled medical practitioners.

A second group felt that skill in written and verbal expression were critical for any professional. If students didn't have these coming in, they should have them when they left. This group tended to view the goal of medical school as the education of professionals — physicians who were skilled practitioners, but also had a broader role as educated members of the community.

To my knowledge, these positions had not been articulated before the workshop. While no agreement was reached, the discussion was spirited. Everyone agreed that the issue needed further attention, and asked me to gather more information for a future workshop.

Goal 2:   Workshops as Image-Building

Choose controversial topics.   The best-attended
workshops have been topics such as a discussion of the "Dr.
Fox" studies (Abrami, Levelthal, and Perry, 1982), a debate
on the value of educational objectives, and a presentation of
research on student ratings of instruction. Attendance at some
workshops has reached 40, including 20-25 of our faculty of
80 and 10-15 members of the professional staff and student
teaching fellows.

Figure 1 shows the text from the invitation to the
workshop, "Entertainment and Education, or Who is Dr. Fox
and what does he know about giving a lecture?".

Few faculty had heard of the "Dr. Fox effect."   I
reviewed the original "Dr. Fox" study and subsequent attempts
to replicate it, presenting weaknesses in the research as well as
findings. I answered questions about the research and the
implications people had drawn from it.

Discussion was lively. The audience was intrigued by
this new light on lecturing. They were particularly interested
in its impact on the validity of student ratings of instruction,
an ongoing debate. Some faculty felt this research proved that
student ratings were invalid. Others saw a need to combine
good speaking skills with required content.

Present alternative viewpoints. Choosing controversial
topics is futile unless you discuss legitimate arguments on
several sides of the issue. These can be structured to reflect
opinions held by members of your audience, or drawn from
current literature. You may have your mind made up, but
failing to represent multiple viewpoints will squash discussion
and reinforce the idea that you have "the right answer."

Figure 2 presents the text from the invitation to the
workshop, "Learning Objectives in Medical Education:
Behavioral, Cognitive, or Trivial?" Everyone had heard of
learning objectives. All three positions described on the flyer
were represented in the audience. I presented contrasting
theories of education relating to learning objectives, reviewed
arguments for and against, and discussed implementation
problems that often led instructors to reject the whole process

(Melton, 1978; Mast, et al., 1980; Williams and Osborne, 1982).

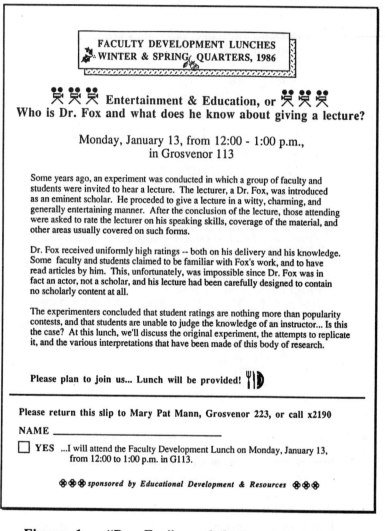

Figure 1. "Dr. Fox" workshop announcement.

```
┌─────────────────────────────────────────────────┐
│   ╔═══════════════════════════════════════╗      │
│   ║  FACULTY DEVELOPMENT LUNCHES          ║      │
│   ║  WINTER & SPRING QUARTERS, 1986       ║      │
│   ╚═══════════════════════════════════════╝      │
```

Learning Objectives in Medical Education:
Behavioral, Cognitive, or Trivial?

Tuesday, February 18, from 12:00 - 1:00 p.m.,
in Grosvenor 113

...There are a variety of "positions" in education regarding objectives --

Some educators feel that providing students with a complete set of behavioral objectives is the only defensible way to teach. They feel that students deserve a clear, specific, and objective statement of what is required of them. Without behavioral objectives, students are reduced to "psyching out" the instuctor to get a grade -- some- thing at which many students are quite adept, but has little to do with the real world.

Others feel that, while there is a role for objectives, behavioral statements are as useless as the behavioristic tradition that spawned them. Behaviorism seems most useful in training those who must learn complicated procedures by heart (like fighter pilots), or those with low level cognitive skills or training (like the mentally retarded). Behavioral objectives are probably most applicable in similar arenas -- certainly not in college or professional school. Cognitive objectives, however, can guide student learning and keep the instructor organized and on target.

Finally, some feel that any kind of objective represents spoon-feeding, and detracts from the independent thought and inquiry that is central to higher education. They squash creativity in the classroom, and are designed as a means to control teachers.

Please plan to join us to discuss these issues... Lunch will be provided!

Please return this slip to Mary Pat Mann, Grosvenor 223, or call x2190

NAME _____

☐ YES ...I will attend the Faculty Development Lunch on Tuesday, February 18, from 12:00 to 1:00 p.m. in G113.

✤✤✤ *sponsored by Educational Development & Resources* ✤✤✤

Figure 2. Learning objectives workshop announcement.

Figure 3 is an example from the "Learning Objectives" workshop, a list of situations in which objectives might be useful or detrimental. I wanted to suggest that different approaches may be needed in different learning situations.

CHARACTERISTICS OF LEARNING SITUATIONS
IN WHICH OBJECTIVES MAY BE:

USEFUL   DETRIMENTAL

psychomotor skills   content which is necessarily
                                or unavoidably ambiguous
cognitive skills or knowledge in
which content has an explicit   discovery learning
structure   approaches

adult learners with   emphasis on problem-
explicit goals   solving or higher-level
                                analytical skills
large amounts of material in
which important points may
be lost

mastery learning, self-instruction,
or competency-based learning

Figure 3. **"Objectives" workshop summary.**

Figure 4 is the concluding overhead for the "Dr. Fox" workshop, which attempts to illustrate both the advantages and drawbacks of the "Dr. Fox effect."

Reviewing conflicting points of view enabled some participants to articulate their views more clearly. Faculty gave examples of how they had used objectives, and the negative and positive impacts of these attempts. Discussion focused on pragmatic issues, chiefly the amount of time involved vs. the benefit to students.

Provide some conclusions. This may seem to contradict the previous points, but most audiences feel uncomfortable when things are left completely up in the air. Educational theory and practice are your areas of expertise. Faculty want to know the current view within the field and, ultimately, your view on the issue. This can be tricky when you have been trying to discuss multiple viewpoints in an open-minded fashion. Rather than presenting hard-and-fast conclusions, I summarize advantages and disadvantages or present criteria for making decisions.

SOME PLAUSIBLE CONCLUSIONS
ABOUT DR. FOX

Instructor "expressiveness," i.e., wit, charm, personality, has an impact on students.

Sometimes, this expressiveness can overshadow what students actually learn from an instructor.

To the extent that ratings should reflect learning, the expressiveness of an instructor can artificially inflate ratings from students.

Δ Student ratings should not be the only measure of an instructor's teaching.

The finding that sometimes expressiveness can mask a lack of content does not mean that instructors who are witty, charming, or good speakers are not serious scholars; or that dull, pedantic presentations are always full of important material.

Expressiveness contributes to a lecture by making it more enjoyable. This can motivate students to attend class, to pay closer attention while in class, and to develop an interest in the topic being presented. These are desirable ends in their own right.

Δ Instructors should be encouraged to develop good speaking skills, but not encouraged to sacrifice coverage of content to present flashy lectures.

Figure 4.   "Dr. Fox" workshop summary.

Goal 3:   Workshops as Forums

The two previous sections provide some examples of *how* to stimulate discussion in workshops. This section discusses *why* faculty discussion can be valuable in professional development programs.

Opportunities to discuss teaching. Faculty don't spend much time talking about their teaching, particularly at universities and larger colleges. Planning and presenting classes, working with students, and evaluating their performance require large amounts of faculty time and effort. Ideas and values related to teaching, however, are seldom addressed.

Workshops provide an informal, low-stress setting in which thoughts about teaching can be expressed and new ideas can be presented. No one can adopt an innovation without hearing about it, so some workshops can be devoted to presenting new things happening within the institution. For example, I've presented a survey of how various faculty are using computers in their courses and invited individual faculty to present their innovations, such as using small-group discussion or independent study formats.

Opportunities to explore diversity. It is surprisingly easy for faculty to become isolated, particularly from colleagues in other departments. This often leads to the formation of stereotypes and reliance on generalizations. The most common form I find is the assumption that "everyone in my area thinks like me and we are right, and everyone in that other area thinks differently and they are wrong."

This summation is oversimplified, of course, but not far from the truth. It tends to be supported by experience because colleagues in your own department will generally not oppose you in public even when they disagree. Opposition to new proposals tends to come from other areas, which often seem to present a united front.

Individual discussions with faculty reveal differences in underlying beliefs and values about education that are reflected in teaching methods. It can be enlightening for faculty to realize that there is a broad range of opinion about a given issue and that the differences are not determined by departmental lines. In addition, it is extremely valuable for educational consultants to hear faculty views and to participate in discussions of pedagogical problems.

Conclusion: The New Workshop and Consultation

The key to developing workshops into individual consultation projects is to provide follow-up. Consulting projects grow from workshops when individual participants are interested enough to ask for more information. A few workshops have led directly to consulting projects, notably the opportunity to develop a computer-assisted case for use in testing and invitations to conduct in-depth evaluations of courses experimenting with innovative methods.

Most requests for follow-up, however, have been brief and focused. After specific workshops, faculty have asked me to review course syllabi, edit test items or class handouts, assist them in preparing goals and objectives, or attend meetings to discuss related issues with faculty groups. Some of these interactions have developed into long-term consulting relationships; many have not. Each gave me an opportunity to learn more about individual faculty members and their needs and interests, to assist them in their teaching, and to demonstrate my skills.

A typical spring workshop schedule includes two "controversial" topics, one traditional topic on test items (included to present recent changes in the test-scoring program), and two opportunities to discuss course innovations (**Figure 5**). All were well attended and generated ample discussion. All resulted in some short-term follow-up (such as reviewing tests or objectives); a few have led to more extensive consulting projects (such as developing a syllabus or evaluating a course).

Workshops remain as a low-cost, highly visible component in professional development programs. The ideas outlined here have helped me develop a workshop program that supported my efforts in individual consultation, increased attendance (compared with past skills-oriented workshops), and renewed my interest in presenting workshops.

References

Abrami, P.C., Leventhal, L., and Perry, R.P. (1982). Educational seduction. *Review of Educational Research, 52*, 446-464.

Mast, T.A., Silber, D.L., Williams, R.G., Evans, G.P. (1980). Medical student use of objectives in basic science and clinical instruction. *Journal of Medical Education, 55*, 65-772.

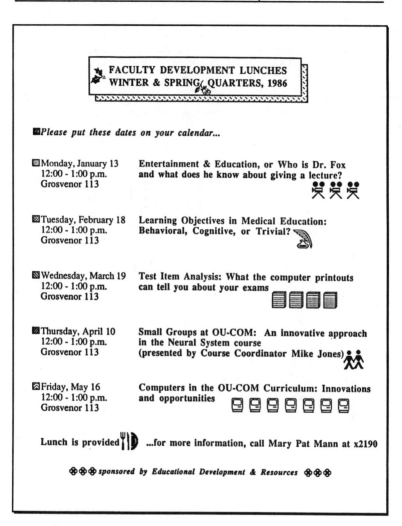

Figure 5. Typical spring workshop schedule.

Melton, R.F. (1978). Resolution of conflicting claims concerning the effect of behavioral objectives on student learning. *Review of Educational Research, 48*, 291-302.

Williams, R.G., and Osborne, C.E. (1982). Medical teachers' perspectives on development and use of objectives. *Medical Education, 16*, 68-71.

Mary Pat Mann is Coordinator for Faculty Development, Athens campus, for the Ohio University College of Osteopathic Medicine. Her academic background is in Anthropology and Instructional Systems Technology and she has been involved in faculty development related activities since 1983. She welcomes comments and suggestions, and can be reached at: 223 Grosvenor Hall, OU College of Osteopathic Medicine, Athens, Ohio 45701, (614) 593-2190.

The Teaching Analysis Program and the Role of the Consultant

Joyce T. Povlacs
Teaching and Learning Center
University of Nebraska-Lincoln

College teachers call on instructional consultants for a variety of reasons. Although their general intent may be to bring about some improvement in teaching and learning in their classes, their motives may vary from displeasure with student evaluations the previous semester to restlessness with their current approaches to teaching. A flexible model for instructional development is needed to address the range of their requests. The Teaching Analysis Program, as offered at the Teaching and Learning Center of the University of Nebraska, provides a basic pattern for instructional improvement and at the same time is sufficiently flexible to meet a variety of needs. In this process the instructional consultant plays a complex, integral part in assisting the faculty member in clarifying goals, gathering and interpreting data, and planning for modification. The intent of this chapter is to describe the Teaching Analysis Program as a model together with some of its variations, offer some observations on the role of the instructional consultant in the process, and give an example of the process at work with a faculty client.

The Teaching Analysis Program

Based on the Teaching Improvement Process developed at the University of Massachusetts-Amherst Clinic to Improve University Teaching, the Teaching Analysis Program, as we designate it, is both a systematic and an individualized approach to improving instruction in the classroom. The program focuses on the improvement of teaching skills, but it is flexible enough to address a variety of concerns in instructional, curricular, or professional development. In conducting Teaching Analysis, the instructional consultant helps the faculty member become aware of the processes of instruction and of the strategies available to increase students' satisfaction and achievement in the classroom.

The Teaching Analysis Program is founded on the theory that feedback on behavior, accompanied by support, produces change in behavior. Student feedback accompanied by consultation has been shown to have a positive impact on student evaluations of instruction (Erickson and Erickson, 1979; Aubrecht, 1979; Stevens and Aleamoni, 1985). The study by Erickson and Erickson (1979) is especially noteworthy here because they made use of the Teaching Improvement Process in their consultation. In reporting their investigations, they conclude:

> ...faculty members who go through the teaching consultation procedure improve their performance of target skills. Moreover...those improvements in teaching are relatively durable. (p.682)

One of the benefits from consultation is that the instructor is able to move from general perceptions about the quality of instruction to focus on specific behavior, teaching methods, or materials to modify.

The Teaching Analysis Program is conducted during the time the course is being taught. The process consists of five phases, and each can have a number of variations, as described below.

1. **Clarifying goals and objectives.** In the initial phase the instructor and the consultant discuss what the instructor is trying to accomplish and how the consultant can be of service. This discussion, often identified as the "initial meeting," is usually held by appointment, after contact has been established.

2. **Data-gathering.** The second phase, which can begin as early as three weeks into the semester, consists of gathering information about the teaching and learning going on in the classroom. The instructor and the consultant agree on how the information is to be gathered. Usually three perspectives are represented: the instructor's, the students', and the consultant's. Methods of collecting data commonly used include conferences between instructor and consultant, examination of course materials, classroom observations, audio- and videotaping, use of the student questionnaire *Teaching Analysis by Students (TABS)*, individual student interviews, and *Small Group Instructional Diagnosis (SGID)*, in which the consultant visits the classroom to gather feedback from small groups (Clark and Bekey, 1979).

3. **Analyzing data and planning.** In the third phase the consultant and the instructor go over the collected information together. In this "data review" meeting, strengths and concerns are identified, and hypotheses accounting for students' opinions are surfaced and evaluated. If the instructor chooses, a plan for testing hypotheses and modifying instruction is developed. The consultant's role in Phase 3 is especially complex as it is comprised of those of a colleague, an active listener, a facilitator, and perhaps an expert. (See discussion of the role of the consultant below.)

4. **Modifying and practicing.** In the fourth phase, the instructor makes the changes as identified above. She or he may share the students' feedback and plans for modification with the class. The class and the instructor thus can take joint responsibility for improving instruction. Modifications may range from writing the day's objectives on the overhead or chalkboard, presenting material on visuals, asking more questions at a variety of cognitive levels, conducting review sessions, and increasing handouts, to producing course manuals and redesigning the course itself.

5. **Evaluating the improvement and the process.** In the final phase, near the end of the course, the instructor may ask students about their awareness of change and their relative satisfaction with the instructional skills. Often the feedback comes as part of the final evaluation of the course, using a departmental or college-wide instrument. The Teaching and Learning Center also asks faculty members to evaluate the Teaching Analysis Program as it has been conducted in the current semester.

The process of the Teaching Analysis Program is both confidential and voluntary. Even though a department chair might strongly encourage a faculty member to seek help, she or he must choose to become involved. All information gathered in the process belongs to the faculty member and is released only by that person. Over the years, we have promoted an environment where it is quite acceptable to be seen talking with the instructional consultant, and our clients often identify themselves to their colleagues as having worked with us. (A complete description of the process of teaching consultation as developed at the University of Massachusetts-Amherst may be found in Bergquist and Phillips, 1977, pp. 69-115.)

Variations on the Model

The Teaching Analysis Program, as outlined above, consists of a clear and logical sequence of gathering information, interpreting that information, modifying instruction, and receiving feedback. In application, however, variations occur from beginning to end.

In the first place, one might well ask where the beginning of the process occurs. For instance, we often get requests to send TABS through the campus mail for faculty members to administer. In such cases, the consultant checks to confirm the request and offers at least to assist in reading the print-out. This offer is usually accepted, and the discussion of the TABS results often does lead into a full process of Teaching Analysis. In this case, the client and the consultant are led inductively to setting goals and clarifying the process of instructional improvement that ordinarily occurs in Phase 1.

Another variation on the model is found in the on-going nature of the intervention. While the methodology of empirical research requires that all data be in before a diagnosis is made, "insights dawn" and hypotheses are posed throughout the process. In practice, discussing with the faculty member the observations I have made in visiting a class while it is fresh in our memory (the next hour if possible) is more useful than waiting several days or a week until all the data are in. Since my style of note-taking in an observation is to write down as much of what I saw and heard as I can, the discussion tends to be a dialog between the two of us about classroom activity. It often elicits immediate insight and thus invites immediate change.

In other cases the data-gathering phase stretches out. If, for instance, the consultant and the faculty member are puzzled over student responses on the TABS questionnaire, the solution may be found in conducting a process of small-group feedback (SGID) in the classroom in order to hear more directly why students think the instruction is not clear, materials not explained well, grading is not fair, or the like. The consultation can also go into a new semester when the process was started too late in the previous one.

In applying the process of Teaching Analysis, many other variables are important and can cause a departure from the model. For instance, is the faculty member a first time client, a new faculty member, or a veteran of Teaching Analysis who might be regarded as on a "maintenance" program? In the last case, the initial interview of Phase 1 may be greatly shortened. Variation also occurs when a faculty member elects to do only part of the process. Often videotaping is not feasible; in other cases, the instructor is not ready for the consultant to visit the class.

Throughout all the phases of the Teaching Analysis Program it is important to remember that the faculty member as the content expert and the instructional consultant who is informed about the principles of teaching and learning work as colleagues to seek solutions to instructional problems. In managing the process for the faculty member, the consultant needs to be aware of the various roles and functions she or he plays.

Role of the Instructional Consultant

The Teaching Analysis Program, as described above, provides a basic model which can be modified to meet the needs of the situation. The instructional consultant therefore assumes a number of roles in identifying and describing the process of teaching and learning and in assisting the faculty member in improving instruction. Some of these roles and the skills the consultant needs are described below.

1. The consultant as colleague.

A review of studies on feedback by Menges and Brinko (1985) reveals that feedback is best received when the consultant is of equal status with the faculty member. "Equal status" might be achieved if the consultant has experience in teaching in higher education and expertise in teaching improvement. A consultant coming from outside the discipline has an advantage over one in the same subject area. When the consultant and the faculty member are in the same discipline, the process can get sidetracked into the speculations and controversies over subject matter and the consultant can lose the perspective of the observer. But even if both are within the same discipline or even the same academic unit, Teaching Analysis can still be conducted, as long as both persons are aware of the pitfalls.

The consultant and the faculty member, acting as colleagues, examine the data together and make decisions, much as two scholars might examine the text of a literary work or a report of an experiment and draw conclusions. Viewed in this manner, the process is regarded, not as remedial, but as collaborative. If the consultancy gets off on this foot, then faculty members will neither allow us to belabor the obvious nor fail to respect their autonomy.

In spite of good intentions, sometimes the faculty member casts the consultant in the role of the authority and demands recipes for effective teaching from the expert. While the consultant can be an expert, she or he can give only guidance in application of instructional principles and strategies. It is important, therefore, to establish early in the consultancy that one is a colleague. I do so in a number of ways, depending on the conversation. These include giving examples out of my own teaching experience; being descriptive and not prescriptive; constantly inviting the faculty member to make choices in the process; asking the faculty member about elements in the subject matter and the rationale for how it is offered; and discussing our mutual concerns for our university and higher education in general. Over the years my clients appear to be most comfortable addressing me by my first name. I usually reciprocate, unless the person exhibits a very formal demeanor or is from another culture. In those cases, I ask what is the preferred form of address.

The collaboration inherent in Teaching Analysis, as colleagues work together to improve instruction, can result in their doing joint presentations on campus and at discipline and teaching conferences and in co-authoring articles and other publications. Although in many helping professions forming friendships is not encouraged, in this case, over the years, faculty colleagues can and do become friends.

2. The consultant as active listener.

One way to be a good colleague is to be a good listener. The consultant, therefore, should be aware of and practice active listening. Active listening is important for a number of reasons: the consultant gains information; the faculty member clarifies and accepts the situation for herself or himself; positive qualities such as mutual trust and increased self-confidence develop; and apprehensions are diminished. The skills of active listening include acceptance of other's feelings (but not necessarily agreement with opinion expressed); empathy or sensing how the other is feeling; probing or asking questions to get at information and attitudes; paraphrasing what has been said for clarity; assisting in listing of options for decisions; and summarizing for closure (Bergquist and Phillips, 1977, p. 207). Non-verbal behavior is also important. I observe the signals the client gives and, at the same time, I am aware of what messages I might send. For instance, frowning in concentration, covert glances at the clock, fiddling with objects on a desk, and even sometimes note-taking can be distracting.

What do instructional consultants listen for? In the initial interview, especially on first contact, I listen to determine why the faculty member has requested services. Sometimes the person has been "sent" by a department chair and hence we will have to decide if the person really wants to engage in Teaching Analysis. Other questions I ask myself as I listen include:

- Is the person generally pleased with teaching? displeased? content or bitter about students and the institution?

- Is there a specific problem or need or just a general notion about improving?

- What does the faculty member know about learning theory, its applications, student characteristics, and strategies of active learning?

While some of this information is elicited by direct questioning, much of the instructor's attitude can be determined by conversing about the teaching assignment and load, past and present; length of service to the university; specializations and aspirations in the discipline; descriptions of typical students, and the like.

Active listening skills are needed throughout the series of conferences one holds in conducting Teaching Analysis. For example, in Phase 3, in the data review meeting, faculty members often express hurt and anger over students' ratings and comments. The consultant must on one hand accept these perfectly normal (and often justified) feelings without diminishing the importance of the feedback. For instance, I often hear myself saying something like this: "Yes, I can understand why you are upset when the students perceive you are disorganized. Can you think of anything that happened which might have caused such a strong response?" Resistance followed by disequilibrium appears to be a pre-requisite for change. By refocusing attention on events in the classroom, we are more likely to discover the cause of the students' negative responses and to make needed changes.

3. The consultant as the facilitator and change agent.

As the guide and manager of the Teaching Analysis Program, the consultant assumes the major role of a facilitator. The ingredients of being a facilitator are many, including the roles already described. Some of the other facilitative tasks include guiding the decision-making process of Teaching Analysis, keeping the process going, describing and analyzing the data, making suggestions or aiding in the listing of alternatives, and involving students in gathering the feedback. Acting as the facilitator prevents one from assuming the role of the authority figure. For example, in the initial meeting a faculty client may pose a problem and wait expectantly for the expert—the consultant—to speak. In this case, I might say something like this: "I cannot say why your students are behaving in the way you describe. In order to gain a better understanding of what is going on, we need to collect some information." At that point I suggest the elements of Teaching Analysis which seem most appropriate, and we come to closure on how and when the data will be gathered.

The consultant is also facilitative by guiding the arrangements for Teaching Analysis. In order to convey to the faculty member that instructional improvement is a normal process of teaching and learning, I suggest that we meet in her or his office. In that way we have convenient access to course materials, and I can observe how the instructor acts on the home turf (reactions to telephone calls and drop-in students, methods of filing instructional materials, office decor, extremes of messiness or tidiness, and so forth). Although I occasionally engage in a marathon session, the most comfortable length of a conference—initial, observation feedback, or data-review—is about an hour. While the faculty member assumes responsibility for making initial contact and for supplying agreed upon information, once an agreement is reached on the process, the consultant takes the lead in setting dates for data-gathering and feedback and monitors the process throughout.

Another way the consultant serves as a facilitator is found in the contact with students. In the data-gathering of Phase 2, the consultant may interview students individually or in small groups in the classroom. In Small Group Instructional Diagnosis (SGID) (Clark and Bekey, 1979), the consultant asks the students to form small groups during the class period, without the instructor's presence; they are asked to decide what's going well and what's not going well and to make a recommendation for improvement. When the groups have completed their discussions, the opinions are reported out accumulatively to the class as a whole. In this process the consultant often serves as a lightening rod, as dissatisfactions are voiced and in conversation defused. Afterwards, the feedback is then shared with the instructor, but that is not the only important result. Frequently after I have conducted SGID in a class, the instructor will tell me that the students are now asking more questions and are much more responsive than they were before my visit. The secret (shared with the client!) is that in gathering the feedback, I talk about the importance of active participation with the students and suggest ways of asking questions and articulating their views in class.

One of the most important ways the consultant serves as the facilitator is in the analysis and interpretation of the data. Throughout the feedback sessions, the consultant is constantly asking questions about expectations, intentions, and feelings as the teaching story unfolds. In data-review conferences, the faculty member and I usually move point by point through my observation notes, the TABS print-out with student commentary, or other collected data. This inductive approach is accompanied by many pauses to hypothesize about what occasioned student responses.

The inductive data review for student feedback is not appropriate if student opinions are in either extreme. If the student data are extremely positive, then I begin by asking the faculty member what items she or he was pleased with in the feedback. We may then discuss a few of the items on TABS rated the highest or some of the written comments. From there, we may move into some areas which were not so strong, or we may discover that while the course appears to be going well, the instructor wants to increase the interaction (often beyond the students' expectations) or change to a new approach altogether. If the student data are largely negative, it is important to find something positive to reinforce, and then concentrate on a few points which appear to be the most significant and the most amenable to change.

In addition to conducting the feedback sessions, the consultant acts as the facilitator in other ways. After data are reviewed, the hypotheses suggested must be tested and plans for change formulated. The consultant facilitates the tasks by supplying necessary resource materials, linking the faculty member to other resources such as an on campus workshop, and committing time to further observation, follow-up, and evaluation. At the end of feedback sessions I often give the faculty member one or more short handouts describing learning principles or effective teaching. Most teachers want to help students increase abilities in problem solving and critical thinking; material on Bloom's taxonomy (Bloom, 1956), developmental levels (Piaget, 1978; Perry, 1970), and characteristics of good teaching (Hildebrand, 1973), as well as on a host of other topics, gives us a common vocabulary about teaching and learning and builds awareness of principles of learning and cognition.

Throughout, I take a proactive role in checking with the faculty member periodically and into the next semester or academic year. Chance meetings in classroom buildings, departmental offices, the cafeteria, and student union are effective ways of keeping in touch with both new and former clients.

Each consultation is unique. The case described below exhibits how a part of Teaching Analysis was used over time to give a faculty member a picture of his teaching and build an awareness of how modifications might improve even an "above average" instructor.

The Case of the Above Average Instructor

Just before spring vacation, I received a telephone call from Mark Young (a pseudonym). I had first met Mark several years ago. He was a young assistant professor fresh out of graduate school who had been hired in a department in one of the applied sciences. He was replacing a popular teacher who had resigned his position with the university and Mark expressed some concern over following in the footsteps of such a well-known and well-liked figure. "I'm not very funny," he said.

The first occasions of our meeting, if I can recall, were at the university's new faculty orientation and, a little later, at the Teaching and Learning Center's seminar on teaching for new faculty. Throughout the first year, while Mark attended some presentations on instructional improvement, he did not indicate further interest in our services. In the second year, he had his first experience with one of the sophomore-level courses taught by the former professor. In October I had a request from him to gather data in that class. In his telephone call that fall, it appeared that running the TABS questionnaire — we settled on the short form TABS B (see **Figure 1**) — was all that he was willing to do at this point. Therefore, I did not press him for the "initial interview" of Phase 1, but we agreed to conduct an interpretation of the results together.

When the TABS print-out together with the students' comments crossed my desk I was surprised to see that his students had given him very high marks. An examination of the first column of data in **Tables 1** and **2** reveals what I first saw. Of the 64 students who filled out TABS B (see **Figure 1**), a combined 80 percent or better rated Mark "good" or "excellent" on 14 to 20 items. Only three items had less than 70 percent on the top two ratings. These items included:

> # 3 - making distinctions between major and minor
>   topics,
> #13 - taking action when students appeared bored, and
> #20 - informing students about their progress in the
>   course.

Students' written comments, which I had grouped according to how students had rated the course (Item #24), also were far more positive than negative. Students praised the instructor's caring attitude, and some liked the materials, the course booklet, and slide presentations. Those students who rated the course lower (Satisfactory, Fair) found some fault with the applications of the subject matter to immediate problems, with testing, and with boredom. Two comments were especially worrisome: one student complained that "The course should be taught as a lecture class, not interactively,"

Items on Teaching Analysis by Students (TABS)
(Form B)

Items #1-20 are marked as follows:
1. No improvement needed (very good or excellent performance)
2. Little improvement needed (generally good performance)
3. Improvement needed (generally mediocre performance)
4. Considerable improvement needed (generally poor performance)

THE INSTRUCTOR'S PERFORMANCE IN . . .

1. making effective use of class time
2. making clear the purposes of each class session and learning activity
3. integrating the various topics treated in the course
4. making clear the distinction between major and minor topics
5. adjusting the rate at which ideas are covered so that I can follow and understand them
6. clarifying material which needs explanation
7. wrapping things up before moving on to a new topic
8. assigning useful readings and homework
9. maintaining an atmosphere which actively encourages learning
10. responding to questions raised by students
11. inspiring excitement or interest in the content of the course
12. using a variety of teaching techniques
13. taking appropriate action if students appear to be bored
14. asking thought-provoking questions
15. getting students to participate in class discussions or activities
16. relating to students in ways which promote mutual respect
17. explaining what is expected from each student
18. making clear precisely how my performance is to be evaluated
19. designing evaluation procedures which are consistent with course goals
20. keeping me informed about how well I am doing

(Figure 1 - con't)

21. How much do you think you are learning so far in this course?
    a. A great deal
    b. A fair amount
    c. Very little
    d. Nothing

22. In your judgment, how important is what you are being asked to learn in this course?
    a. Very important
    b. Somewhat important
    c. Not very important
    d. Not at all important

23. In comparison to other instructors you have had (in high school and college), how do you rate the effectiveness of this instructor?
    a. One of the most effective (top 10%)
    b. More effective than most (top 30%)
    c. About average (middle 40%)
    d. Not as effective as most (lower 30%)
    e. One of the least effective (lowest 10%)

24. So far, what is your overall rating of this course?
    a. Excellent
    b. Good
    c. Satisfactory
    d. Fair
    e. Poor

25. In answering question number 24, what made you rate the course as high as you did and/or what kept you from rating the course higher? Please make your remarks on Written Comments sheet.

SOURCE: From the Teaching Analysis by Students (TABS) of the Clinic to Improve University Teaching, University of Massachusetts at Amherst (1974) and TABS B from the Instructional Development Program, University of Rhode Island, as modified by the Teaching and Learning Center, University of Nebraska-Lincoln.

Figure 1. Short form, TABS B.

and another said "Would rather take my own notes instead of trying to keep track of where we are and skipping around in the manual." These two comments and one more (all by students who rated the course only Satisfactory or Fair) gave some indication of areas for concern. The third comment, made by someone who rated the course as "Fair," read: "I rated it lower because I don't think sufficient information is

Table 1

TABS B Data for Three Reports

Mark Young's Course
Fall 1985, Spring 1986, Spring 1987

Percentage of Students Marking 1 + 2
(Excellent or Good)

TABS B Item		Fall'85 (n=64) %	Spr'86 (n=50) %	Spr'87 (n=50) %
1.	Classtime	96.8	96.0	100.0
2.	Purpose	82.5	78.0	96.0
3.	Integration	87.3	60.0	94.0
4.	Major/Minor	50.7	48.0	50.0
5.	Rate	73.0	76.0	82.0
6.	Clarifying	78.2	82.0	94.0
7.	Wrap Up	84.4	82.0	88.0
8.	Readings/Homework	82.6	87.7	86.0
9.	Active Learning	82.5	84.0	88.0
10.	Responding to Questions	93.8	98.0	94.0
11.	Excitement	74.6	71.4	66.0
12.	Variety	81.0	65.3	76.0
13.	Boredom	53.1	40.8	48.9
14.	Thought-Provoking	90.5	81.7	80.0
15.	Participating	88.7	79.6	88.0
16.	Respect	92.1	93.9	96.0
17.	Work Expected	81.0	81.6	84.0
18.	How Evaluated	85.3	83.7	86.0
19.	Consistent	90.7	83.6	90.0
20.	Informed	66.2	81.6	86.0

given over each subject area. Important facts aren't always stated and note taking is difficult."

Having highlighted the strengths and some of the concerns for myself, I sat down with Mark for our first feedback session in his office. I cannot recall much of the conversation that day, but we did spend time getting acquainted and I learned that Mark did indeed want to increase the interaction in his classes. We briefly touched on the problem of students who do not want interaction, and I suggested some ways to improve the students' awareness of course and lecture organization. Mark told me that because he was new to the course, he still needed to prepare material that made the applications the students wanted. He did not anticipate being able to augment and overhaul his materials and the course manual until summer, however. We acknowledged that new materials could well give more excitement to the course. Because the TABS and written comments appeared so positive, I did not suggest any further data gathering this semester and we parted without further plans to meet at this point.

Mark called me early the following semester. He had received his end-of-course ratings for the course and was not at all pleased. This time we set an appointment and a true Phase 1, "initial interview" was conducted. The ratings, I

Table 2

Means for TABS B Items 21, 22, 23, 24

Mark Young's Course
Fall 1985, Spring 1986, Spring 1987

Scale 1 = High

	Item	Fall'85 (n=64)	Spr'86 (n=50)	Spr'87 (n=50)	
21.	Amount Learned	1.94	1.94	1.68	(4 pt. scale)
22.	Importance	1.42	1.49	1.46	(4 pt. scale)
23.	Instructor	2.22	2.34	2.12	(5 pt. scale)
24.	Course	2.21	2.26	2.04	(5 pt. scale)

recall, were not especially low, but his department was noted for its good teaching and he wanted to be among the top. He also once again expressed concern that his personality was unexciting and hence his students would see him and the course as "dry and boring." At this point, I noted that we needed to collect data from the students in the current semester — he was teaching the same course again — and that I needed to get a feel for his teaching style and to watch for the interactions in the classroom. We arranged for another administration of TABS B and an observation.

Unfortunately, almost all records of that data-gathering have disappeared. My notes from the classroom observation, which were handed to Mark during the data review, are no longer available, but my impression was of a traditional lecture presentation, some use of the overhead projector, and some question and answer. Mark had a pleasant style about him, but he was not, as he freely admitted, a charismatic figure. The TABS data (still extant) revealed less satisfaction with organization of the course (see **Table 1**, column 2, items #2, #3, #4), and with interest (items #11, #12, #13, #14, and #15) than that expressed the previous semester. Nevertheless 12 items still remained with 80 percent or more rating the course "excellent" or "good." Although we talked about specific modifications for the current semester, I recall only that the main plan of action was for him to spend time during the summer reworking the course material and course manual. This time I was reluctant to leave it at that, but I judged that pressing for more active modification and follow-up was not appropriate. Mark really needed that chance to work on course material.

Matters were pretty much left lying, as far as I knew, until the phone call this spring, an entire year later. In the intervening time I had seen Mark at various workshops and he had consulted with me regarding plans for a small senior seminar and the best methods of gathering student feedback when it finished in December. Also he had been one of several faculty members from his college whom the dean had sent to a special workshop on a new mode of inquiry and teaching interdisciplinary problem-solving. He was applying some of the strategies he had learned at the workshop in his small seminar, and I could anticipate that he was ready to take another look at the course we had been working on.

Over the telephone Mark told me that he wanted to collect data using the TABS B questionnaire again. After spring break, he administered the questionnaire and we met to discuss the results. Evidence in the TABS B data, written comments, and in Mark's comments indicated that Mark was indeed trying new approaches. The materials had been augmented and the course manual revised. He was giving his students more sample problems. Mark had tried a small group problem-solving exercise in class, and he had experienced good results with it.

The data from TABS B (see the third column, **Table 1**, p. 95) exhibited some gains as well as regaining of ground lost. Altogether, 16 items were now being rated "excellent" or "good" by a combined 80 percent of the respondents. The written comments showed some refreshingly motivated students. One student, who rated the course "good," remarked: "My interest in the class subjects was minimal, but now I find myself looking out for things gone over in class. My interest now is up."

There was still a downside for Mark, however. The students were still too passive. And he greatly deplored the low ratings on items #11 and #13 — boredom and excitement (**Table 1**, p. 95). Again some students found the organization "vague." He still wanted to raise his overall instructor evaluation (see **Table 2, item #23**), which he still considered too low. He had shared the results with the class already and he planned some other minor adjustments, but the main questions were yet unresolved. This time we discussed ways to increase student participation and applications of interdisciplinary methods he might use. The end of the semester was once more upon us, and I left him pondering a further course of action.

When I checked with him this summer, he said that he would soon be ready to talk about the next step — and it sounded like a big one. He told me that he wants to organize the material into weekly units. The course, which meets three times a week, will have an introductory lecture the first day of the week it meets, a problem or case to solve the second time, and class discussion and clarification on the third. He is not going to worry about "subject matter coverage," he says, but will indicate clearly what the principles to be learned are and to indicate where these may be found in the reading materials. At this point — the current moment — I plan to intervene once more.

What will that intervention be? In reflecting over the past experiences, I realize that Mark has not needed a major intervention in his teaching as long as he was satisfied in being a better traditional lecturer. He was both knowledgeable about and interested in applying a variety of instructional strategies, but we had defined issues in the framework of the standard lecture course. He once remarked to me that he came out of a group of graduate students in his discipline (which is heavily research-oriented) who enjoy teaching and sought out ways to improve it. It was clear from the outset that Mark would move to his own tune and moreover that he was capable of doing so. The role I had played was that of an active listener and colleague.

Some persons might suggest that no further intervention is needed. Mark, after all, is one of those persons who do not "need" the services of an instructional consultant. There are many who indeed need more help than he did — and I have worked with these too — but Mark is worthy of more time spent. I want to work with Mark because I see him now ready to abandon the traditional lecture pattern and take risks with almost radical strategies, even in the face of resistance from passive students. Mark's typical lecture course can become a showcase for active learning for others in his department and his college.

To repeat, what should my intervention be? I have several in mind. In conference we should explore the risks and the compensations. We should look at student learning styles (he is familiar with Kolb, 1976, and the Myers-Briggs Type Indicator, 1984) and the implications these have for his approach. I want to check his perceptions of the students' entry skills and their level of motivation. I want to look over his shoulder as he designs his units. I might remind him of material I gave him before on "Guided Design" (Wales and Stager, 1982). I want him to confront the major and minor topic issue once more and pinpoint where his new design will help solve that problem. I also want to see where it answers the need for variety and excitement. Finally, we will want to look at some methods of measuring achievement.

We will, in short, move through the process of Teaching Analysis once again. In our Phase 1 initial meeting, I will also suggest that we gather information at the beginning of the class on students' attitudes and then later on their attitudes toward the new unit design. We also need to find out if the new method not only solves questions of boredom and excitement, but also if these students are actively learning and increasing their problem-solving capacity. Data-gathering might include administering a short specially-designed questionnaire at the beginning of the course, by observing the sequence of three classes and discussing observations, using TABS for student feedback, and, if puzzles still exist, Small Group Instructional Diagnosis. During this process I will also check Mark's teaching behaviors. How does he make the shift from lecturer to facilitator? What kinds of questioning skills does he now exhibit? Can he get students to talk to each other instead of the usual teacher-student exchange? The answers to these questions and others, supplied in Phases 2 and 3, will determine the further course of action for both of us.

I have described Mark Young as an "above average" instructor, in the Lake Wobegone voice of understatement. Mark is certainly concerned and aware of instructional issues and is creative in solving them to further student learning in his courses. Although I did not spend a great deal of time with Mark, his case illustrates how the basic cycle of data-gathering, feedback, and change, even as it is modified from the original Teaching Improvement Process, can be a valuable source for structured feedback and motivation for change for an instructor.

References

Aubrecht, J.D. (1979). Are student ratings of teacher effectiveness valid? *IDEA Paper* , No.2. Manhattan, KS: Center for Faculty Evaluation and Development.

Bergquist, W.H. and Phillips, S.R. (1977). *A handbook for faculty development* (Vol. 2). Washington, D.C.: Council for Advancement of Small Colleges (now Council of Independent Colleges).

Bloom, B.S. (1956). *Taxonomy of educational objectives, handbook 1: Cognitive domain.* New York: David McKay Company, Inc.

Briggs, K.C. and Myers, I.B. (1984). *Myers-Briggs type indicator,* Palo Alto, CA: Consulting Psychologists Press.

Clark, J. and Bekey, J. (1979). Use of small groups in instructional evaluation. *POD Quarterly. 1,* 87-95.

Erickson, G.R. and Erickson, B.L. (1979). Improving college teaching: An evaluation of a teaching consultation procedure. *Journal of Higher Education. 50,* 670-683.

Hildebrand, M. (1973). The character and skill of the effective professor. *Journal of Higher Education. 44,* 41-50.

Kolb, D. (1976). *Learning-style inventory.* Boston, MA: McBer and Company.

Menges, R. and Brinko, K. (1985). Feedback on teaching. A presentation at the Annual Conference of the Professional and Organizational Network in Higher Education. Delavan, WI.

Perry, W.G. *Forms of intellectual and ethical development in the college years: A scheme.* New York: Holt, Rinehart & Winston.

Piaget, J. (1978). In Wadsworth, B. *Piaget for the classroom teacher.* New York: Wadsworth.

Stevens, J.J. and Aleamoni, L.M. (1985). The use of evaluative feedback for instructional improvement: a longitudinal perspective. *Instructional Science. 13,* 285-304.

Wales, C.E. and Stager, R.A. (1982). *Guided Design.* Morgantown, WV: West Virginia University, Center for Guided Design.

Joyce T. Povlacs is an instructional consultant at the Teaching & Learning Center and an Assistant Professor of Agricultural Communications at the University of Nebraska - Lincoln. Her academic background is in English and she has been in Faculty Development related activities since 1976. She welcomes comments and suggestions and can be reached at: Teaching & Learning Center, 121 Benton Hall, University of Nebraska-Lincoln, Lincoln, NE 68588. (402) 472-3079

The Faculty Visitor Program: Helping Teachers See Themselves

Barbara Helling
Diane Kuhlmann
Teaching Learning Center
St. Olaf College

Faculty development at St. Olaf College includes support for traditional individual activities such as sabbaticals and travel to professional meetings, grants to pursue scholarly or curricular projects, and group activities such as workshops on teaching and seminars in which academic and research interests are shared. In addition we have introduced the Faculty Visitor Program which provides any interested teacher with an opportunity to take a look at himself or herself actually teaching in the classroom.

Background

Although the Faculty Visitor Program offers a number of possibilities, including videotaping of classes and peer visits, the element that has been most used has been the opportunity to have a trained student observer. This program began in the fall of 1977 as one element in a faculty development proposal supported by the Andrew W. Mellon Foundation. It arose out of Barbara Helling's Danforth Faculty Fellowship in 1975-76 which focused on developing a new way of observing teachers in classrooms. In contrast to the usual reliance on administrative carrot and stick, the intent was to use social science knowledge about motivating and changing behavior to provide positive support and encouragement to the teacher. Cleveland State University's system of using student observers (Casper and Carroll, 1973), though it operated out of a quite different philosophy, provided the idea for St. Olaf's variation. Similar programs which have existed at neighboring Carleton College and at Dickinson University (Laws, 1977) have also contributed ideas.

Purpose

Basic to St. Olaf's program is the idea that the observer provides information rather than criticism. Many classroom observation systems seem to operate on the assumption that the observer is going to tell the teacher what he or she is doing wrong. We begin with the assumption that the teacher sets the goals and objectives for the class and is therefore the appropriate person to make judgments. The observer not only provides a "student's eye view" but assists the teacher in seeing and understanding what is happening in the classroom. Observation reveals how and when the goals and objectives are being met, and if adjustments are made, what the effects are. The purpose is to enable the teacher to compare his or her intent with actual student experience, helping the teacher decide whether or not to change, how to change, and whether the change is working.

Roles and Participation

Faculty

Faculty participation in the program is voluntary. No one is identified as a "poor" teacher. The assumption is that all of us have things about our teaching which we feel could be improved. Early participants tended to be confident teachers wanting to do some "fine tuning." Because they reported the experience to be safe and helpful, we now work with all kinds of teachers including some with serious problems and poor student evaluations. No one is turned down except for time and budget limitations, and the rule is generally first come first served.

Over the nine years this program has been in operation 82 people out of a faculty of approximately 220 have used a student observer at least once. Of these more than two-thirds remain at St. Olaf. Although the largest number of participants have been untenured people in their early years of teaching, more than a quarter have been associate and full professors with an average of fifteen years of teaching at St. Olaf.

The opportunity is announced in the weekly campus newsletter and the Teaching Learning Center *Courier* but the most persuasive recruiting appears to be done by word of mouth, those who have used a student observer personally recommending it to others. To encourage this communication we offer a lunch session each semester in which teams of teacher and observer are present to talk about their experience. We have also sent letters to department chairs asking them to remind faculty members of the program.

Coordinator

The program is directed by a faculty member who receives one course released time per year to oversee the Teaching Learning Center. In addition to other TLC responsibilities, the Coordinator recruits faculty and student participants, assigns observers to faculty, trains and supervises observers, and consults with participating faculty as requested. We encourage a meeting early in the semester between the coordinator and the teacher-observer team to answer questions and generate ideas about how to get started and how and where to focus. The coordinator's work takes about half the released time or an average of three or four hours a week though the load is heaviest at the beginning of the semester, lightest in the middle.

Students

Candidates for observers are obtained by recommendation from faculty members who have participated in the program. We have found that the experience makes people sensitive to the qualities of a good observer. Those recommended are invited for interview by the coordinator who looks for students who want to be helpful and supportive rather than critical. A student who says, "There are a lot of teachers around here who need straightening out," is probably not a good candidate for this program. In fact, most interviewees want to know how the faculty participants have been selected and are relieved to find that they are volunteers rather than having been identified as problems.

Students are matched to faculty on the basis of schedule, obviously, and other qualifications depending on what the faculty member needs. For an advanced course the observer will probably have to have the same prerequisites as the members of the class. In some cases, however, if the faculty member's intention is to focus on classroom atmosphere or student participation rather than on content it may be possible to select an observer with little background in the subject. Where possible, personal qualities are taken into account so that a confident and assertive observer will not overwhelm a more softspoken and insecure teacher, or vice versa.

The Process

Observation begins as early in the term as assignments can be made. The observer is always expected to talk to the teacher about the purpose of observation before attending class for the first time. The observer attends on the same basis as students enrolled in the class. Observer and teacher meet regularly (at least once a week) to talk about the questions the teacher has and what is to be observed, and to compare notes about what happens in class sessions. Students are paid for the time spent in class, in conferring with the faculty member, and in weekly training sessions. The rate of pay is the same as for other student work on campus.

Training

Students meet once a week as a group with the coordinator. Early sessions include introducing students to a variety of instruments for recording classroom observation, a main purpose being to broaden their understanding of the wide variety of formats in which "good" classes come as well as to suggest techniques and topics for observation. Observers also learn about how to provide useful feedback. Role playing has proved to be a useful training activity. After viewing videotapes of classes at other institutions, one trainee takes the part of the instructor they have seen on the tape while another plays observer. Playing the role of the observer provides practice in wording comments constructively. Having to respond as the teacher to comments from an observer proves very effective in making the students aware of a teacher's sensitivity and potential defensiveness.

Later on, training sessions consist mostly of discussion of the kinds of things observers are encountering. Observers often share ideas of how to be helpful in a particular situation and the coordinator makes suggestions and provides readings which observer and instructor may use together. Observers find these sessions useful in "letting off steam" since they are otherwise expected to maintain strict confidentiality.

Observers are instructed to describe specific behaviors rather than make general comments (for example, "interesting," "confusing") because description conveys more useful information. It is often helpful for teacher and observer to identify a particular behavior and have the observer count the frequency or record the time spent as the teacher works on increasing (for example, waiting after asking a question) or decreasing (for example, overuse of a particular phrase) the behavior. Observers are especially encouraged to look for and comment on the effective or potentially effective things the teacher does. Particularly useful in supporting this positive approach is a checklist of 270 "good teaching behaviors" extracted from the literature on college teaching (Helling, 1975). The intent of focusing on effective behavior is to help teachers see what they do well, learn to build on strengths, and use their own best teaching as a model to strive for all the time.

Some evaluation is always implicit, then, but if the teacher establishes the goals and criteria and determines the focus of the observation, the student can comment with some confidence on the congruence or lack of it between the instructor's behavior and goals without exceeding his or her own expertise.

Faculty use of observer

Sometimes faculty complain that the observer is reluctant to make negative comments. Teachers seem to feel that negative information is the only *real* information. During early meetings with observers they ask, "Was that awful?" or "What was the matter with that?" Observers learn to return the responsibility to the teacher with a question of their own about where or why the teacher perceived a problem. Thus the instructor is encouraged to think carefully about teaching goals and process and to come up with ideas about what the observer might look for.

Perhaps the most difficult part of the program is clarification on the part of the instructor of how he or she wishes to use the observer. Voluntary participants are not problem teachers but they are not perfect teachers either. In some cases they may have identified some questions they wish to ask, certain things they wish to work on or change, but in many cases they are simply troubled by a feeling that they are not teaching as well as they might and they enter the program with the idea that an observer will identify the problem for them. As mentioned above, we do not believe that the student can legitimately do that and it often takes some time for the faculty member to realize that this is the case. Reports of the programs at Cleveland State and at Dickinson seem to indicate that most of the help received from students focuses on the mechanics of teaching, perhaps because this is the area in which student observer and teacher most easily agree that the student can judge. On some of the harder questions of content, organization, and mode of presentation the teacher really must decide what should be observed, direct the observer's activities, and interpret the results. As the observer comes to understand the instructor's goals he or she may become more active in the entire process.

Specifying the questions to be asked of the observer is often difficult. It takes time to move from "Am I being clear?" to focused questions like "What can I do to make clear the importance of idea A?" or "...the transition from idea A to idea B?" These are content questions. Many teachers have difficulty in generating non-content-related questions beyond "Can you hear?," "Can you read what I write on the board?" or in recognizing that it is *inappropriate* for them to ask the observer such questions as "What can I do to increase student interest in the topic?" or "How can I involve students in more active learning in the classroom?" (The students do not have the expertise to answer such questions so, when they come up, faculty members are encouraged to call on one of the professionals in the Teaching Learning Center.)

An advantage of using student observers is that they can be present for every class rather than just the occasional visit which a colleague is likely to have time for. The teacher becomes accustomed to the observer's presence; the observer develops a real sense of what this class is like from day to day and can distinguish between a chance occurrence and a consistent practice. As the semester proceeds, the observer monitors the teacher's progress in implementing modifications, and the observer's presence keeps the teacher working at it. By the end of the term there has been enough practice so that the desired behavior is likely to continue.

Outcomes

It is difficult to specify the impact of this program because the outcomes are very different from one participant to the next. Certainly one common outcome for the student observers is a changed attitude toward their teachers as a result of this new relationship with a particular teacher. As one student said in a written evaluation at the end of the semester,

> Participating in the program helped me personally to pay closer attention to teaching methods of professors in my other classes and helped me to be more understanding, in fact more patient with classroom situations that weren't going well. Even more importantly it gave me a greater sense of responsibility to communicate more closely with instructors—the usefulness both for them and for the student of going in and talking with them about problems or good things happening in classroom situations in their courses made me feel less hesitant about doing so if the teacher seemed at all receptive to it.

Students seem to get great satisfaction out of being helpful. They sometimes worry about not having enough to say after a particular observation session but they can be reassured that their effectiveness is often in causing the teacher to anticipate a comment and make the adjustments in advance.

For faculty participants outcomes may be specific changes in teaching practice, such as regularly allowing time for questions rather than promising time and then letting the lecture run till the bell rings, or regularly including a summary at the end of class or at the beginning of the next class period. One faculty member may broaden his or her repertoire of ways of encouraging student participation. Another may work on mannerisms, while still another revises a course in major ways. Sometimes a participant discovers unexpected student perceptions of himself or herself which leads to rethinking goals or modifying style, or perhaps to more careful explanation to students about what to expect. For some participants the real outcome of a semester's work is discovering the questions one would like to ask, and several participants have used an observer a second time.

The purpose of the Faculty Visitor Program is to assist the teacher in improving his or her own teaching in self-chosen directions. It is in no sense an evaluation as far as the college is concerned. Confidentiality is as complete as the individual faculty member wishes it to be. The coordinator or the observer may point out that some participants have found it useful to introduce the observer to the class and invite students to discuss the class with the observer if they wish. Many choose to do so. Many also talk about their experience in the program to colleagues. However no records are kept beyond the names of teacher-observer teams. No information is provided for salary, tenure, or promotion decisions unless the individual chooses to include in a dossier his or her own description of the experience and what was learned from it. The spirit of the program is helping good, concerned teachers to be even better.

Regardless of specific outcomes, faculty participants generally agree about the helpfulness of having someone to talk to about what goes on in the classroom, of having the stimulus to articulate what is to be accomplished and to make specific connections between those objectives and what happens in the particular class session. Many of the student-teacher teams seem to develop a real feeling of joint responsibility with the student becoming an ally of the teacher in attempting to accomplish certain teaching goals.

Evidence of success

The Faculty Visitor Program at St. Olaf has succeeded in providing for interested faculty an opportunity to examine their classroom teaching privately yet with the semester-long assistance of an intelligent, informed, and supportive person. We are convinced that this kind of non-threatening, controllable, long-term feedback is an effective way of motivating faculty to work on their teaching in meaningful ways, and that trained students can indeed provide such feedback.

An Instructor's Experience

In 1981 I was a new faculty member at St. Olaf, teaching accounting courses. I soon learned that I needed to give additional attention to my instruction. I had heard of the Classroom Visitor Program administered by the Teaching-Learning Center and turned to it for help.

My primary motivation for using a student observer was to assist me in making the transition from teaching at a public university to teaching at a small, selective liberal arts college. At the public university, I taught accounting to accounting majors in a school of business. At the private, liberal arts college I teach in an economics department. None of my students are accounting majors, and very few of them will take more than one accounting course. At the university, the coursework was in large part aimed at preparing students to become certified public accountants; at the liberal arts college, perhaps one student every two years will decide to become a certified public accountant.

When I made the transition between institutions, I had to restructure the material covered in my classes, the emphasis given to the material covered, and even the type of examinations given. I also found it necessary to alter the pace of my classes. At the public university I had a number of superb students, but every class would include a significant number of students who were ill-prepared to handle the mathematics in accounting; for many students at the public university, accounting was one of their most difficult courses. At the private school, I do not have any students with insufficient background in mathematics as preparation for accounting; rather than being one of the more difficult courses in their schedules, accounting is seen as a relatively easy course.

Another adjustment came with my concern for my student ratings. Previously, I had always received excellent student ratings. While I was still finding my student ratings to be above average, they were not outstanding in my new situation. I was not sure if this decline in student ratings was due to my failure to adjust to the new academic environment or if it was because I was no longer teaching accounting to accounting majors, but to students with a more limited interest in the subject matter.

How I Learned of the Program

I became aware of the student observer program from my involvement with the Teaching Learning Center (TLC) on campus. I was introduced to the TLC as part of new faculty orientation and began to participate in various noon luncheons and afternoon seminars the TLC staff offered. I learned of the existence of the student observer program from my participation in the TLC, but actually decided to enter the program after reading about the program in the TLC newsletter.

Selecting an Observer

When I decided to use a student observer, I was asked whether I required a student who had previously taken accounting or if a trained observer with no previous accounting experience would be acceptable. My first inclination was to request a student with experience in accounting. It seemed logical that if someone were to evaluate a class, she should understand the subject matter. However, because none of the available observers had any accounting experience, I was forced to rethink my requirements. As I reconsidered what I really wanted from a student observer, I realized previous accounting experience was not necessary. In fact, after having used the observer, I believe that if the observer had had extensive accounting experience, she would have been less able to provide me with the feedback I desired. Since my major concern was whether the pace of my introductory class was appropriate, the lack of previous experience by my observer was a strength. An experienced accounting student already familiar with the material may actually have had difficulty judging whether the class was moving too quickly. My student observer was a junior education major training to teach German to high school students.

My Observer in the Classroom

My student observer assumed the role of a regular member of the class, but sat in the back of the classroom so she could unobtrusively observe the rest of the class. Since there were over forty students in the class, most students did not even notice that she was not a typical student. I felt it was important for her to be thought of as an ordinary member of the class and to sit in a position in which she could observe class dynamics, because I wanted her to give me feedback about student reactions to my teaching. During the final week of class, I introduced her and explained her function to the class. I then left the classroom a few minutes early and had her collect comments from the students about the class.

Communicating with My Observer

My student observer and I met for one half hour once a week throughout the semester. We began the session with my impressions about the past week's classes followed by her insights. Often her review of the class was more favorable than mine. Next, we would discuss some specific area that she was observing (e.g., the pace of the class). At the end of the session we would discuss any new behavior she had noticed during the past week and set goals for the next week's classes. As the semester progressed, we began to examine a much broader range of issues than I had originally envisioned when I requested an observer. Like many college instructors, I have not had any formal coursework in pedagogy. My student observer introduced me to the discipline of educational theory which has resulted in my becoming more interested in how I can become a more effective teacher.

What I Learned from My Student Observer

The comments from my student observer fell into the following six areas: pace of the course, use of the blackboard, value of preview, administration of quizzes, adherence to the dates on the syllabus, and use of humor as part of my teaching style. I specifically requested that my student observer comment on the pace of the course; the remaining five areas were discovered through asking her to mention anything that added or detracted from the effectiveness of my teaching.

Pace of the course. My observer believed that if she could follow the lecture, the pace was not too rapid. By observing whether the students were taking notes and listening to their comments before and after class, she could determine whether the material was being presented at an appropriate speed.

Another major concern I had was whether the students' blank stares meant confusion or boredom. She determined that often the blank stare was caused by external forces (e.g., beautiful weather or an exam in their next class) over which I had little control or influence.

Use of the blackboard. I used the blackboard almost continually during class; most accounting problems and examples are presented on the board. The observer noted that I was using the blackboard to highlight and illustrate the major topics, but I often used the blackboard in a confusing fashion. I tended to start in the middle and work my way out to the ends erasing material as I went along. The observer made the simple, but extremely effective suggestion that I start on the left hand side of the board and work to the right hand side. When I reach the right hand side (after asking if there are any questions and if anyone still needs the material on the board), I erase the entire board and begin again on the left side.

Taking the time to erase the entire board accomplishes two objectives. First, it prevents students from confusing an earlier example with a later example. Second, while I am erasing the board, the students have the opportunity to finish any additional comments they wish to include in their notes.

Use of preview technique. I generally include a brief outline of the topics to be covered during the hour in the upper left hand corner of the blackboard. Since I have never received any feedback from students about the usefulness of this outline, I became remiss in referring to it during class.

The observer noted that students always included this outline in their notes. She felt that the outline clarified the topics covered in class and encouraged me to refer to the outline during class. She also suggested as an effective conclusion to class, I could refer to the outline and summarize the major points covered.

Administration of quizzes. During the semester, I give several unannounced quizzes. These quizzes are usually administered at the end of the hour to limit the amount of class time devoted to taking examinations. I did not realize, however, that when I walk into the classroom with quizzes, the majority of students spend the rest of the hour furtively studying for the quiz rather than listening to the lecture. The student observer suggested that I either administer the quiz at the beginning of the hour or somehow disguise the bundle of quizzes so the students will not realize that a surprise quiz will be given.

Adherence to the syllabus. My course syllabus and outline previously included specific dates on which topics would be covered and when homework was due. In the first weeks of class I always emphasized that these dates were tentative and subject to change. The observer noted that students had difficulty dealing with this uncertainty, and would prefer that I follow the dates on the outline. While I appreciate the students' desire for certainty, I cannot effectively teach a class if I am tied to a rigid timetable. Instead of changing my lectures to agree consistently with the syllabus, I have instead changed my syllabus to include fewer detailed dates.

Humor as part of my teaching style. While I have always found accounting to be an interesting subject, family and friends have indicated that mine is a minority opinion. Since I am aware that many students are actually afraid of accounting, I try to make the lectures interesting and non-threatening, often by using humor. However, I worry that I may use too much humor or that the humor might detract from the subject matter. The student observer indicated that my use of humor was a strength rather than a weakness, and I should try to use it more frequently.

In the above discussion of the results of my use of a student observer, I hoped to indicate the broad array of information I gained during that semester. I also think it is important to note that much of what I learned was not included in my original goals in using a student observer. At the beginning of the semester, I would not have known to ask about my use of the blackboard — I had absolutely no idea that it was confusing. Another important advantage of my use of a student observer was that I was able to consult with her over a period of time. She became familiar with my personality and my strengths and weaknesses as an instructor. Having her in my class over an entire semester was also useful because not only could she indicate areas that could be changed (for example, my use of the blackboard), she could also observe whether I had successfully incorporated the changes.

Student Observer versus the Faculty Observer

In the above paragraphs, I discussed how useful my student observer had been in improving my teaching style, but could even better results be obtained by using a faculty observer instead of a student? The major problem with using a colleague is often he or she is observing class as part of an adversarial situation such as tenure or salary review. Even if the faculty observer is on friendly terms with the teacher, he or she is there to judge one's performance while the student observer is in the classroom to help one become a more effective instructor.

A more important weakness of colleague observation is that it is non-representative because generally only one class period is observed. The student observer attends class throughout the semester and has the opportunity to see both the best and worst aspects of the class. Also, since the student observer is available throughout the semester, he or she is able to provide feedback on any changes implemented.

Finally, some information which is available to student observers is unavailable to the faculty observer. A faculty member cannot be inconspicuous in the classroom. Students are likely to alter their behavior because they are aware they are being observed.

Student Observer versus the Professional Observer

Shortly after I had my student observer, our department obtained a separate and unrelated grant for a series of pedagogy workshops. As part of the grant I was also able to have a trained educational consultant observe one of my classes. While her comments were very useful and informative, they did not supplant the student observer. The educational consultant had superior knowledge of educational theory, but since she was considerably more expensive, I could only have her observe one class. The major advantage of using the student observer was I could have her attend every class for an entire semester. Another comparative advantage of using a student observer is that she was "just a student"; therefore, she could observe the students without their realizing they were being observed. During one of my weekly meetings with my student observer, I expressed concern that my last lecture had been unclear because the students were extremely unresponsive. My student observer did not feel the clarity of my lecture was the problem. Before class my student observer overheard a number of students discussing the statistics exam which was scheduled for the following hour. She noticed that during my accounting lecture a substantial portion of the class was actually studying for the statistics midterm.

Combining a student observer with an educational consultant could result in a very effective program. The educational consultant could initially observe the class to identify problem areas which the student observer would then follow for the remainder of the semester.

Hints for a Good Experience with a Student Observer

My use of a student observer was extremely valuable because the observation was carefully planned and supervised. The following are suggestions to ensure a worthwhile experience:

1. *The faculty member must have objectives for using the observer.* The goals of the faculty member will determine which student observer will be selected. If an advanced

class is being observed, the student observer may need to have taken the prerequisites for the advanced course, while a student observing an introductory class will probably not need any previous experience in the academic area. The instructor should also set objectives so the observer has specific guidelines for the types of teaching behavior to be observed.

2. *The faculty member must be open to criticism.* In the initial meeting with the observer, the instructor should accept criticism gracefully. A hostile attitude towards criticism may cause the student to withhold any negative observations, and thereby limit the effectiveness of the observations.

3. *The instructor and student observer should meet regularly.* Since both the instructor and student have other demands on their time, it is important to schedule a regular time to meet and discuss the class. Regular feedback during the semester is the most valuable aspect of using a student observer.

In the Future

It has been two years since I had a student observer in my classroom. At some point in the near future, I would like to have another observer. I am currently trying to find a more effective method of handling homework assignments in my accounting classes. Over a semester, I would like to try a number of different methods of discussing homework, and have the student observer comment on student reactions to these methods. I also find myself at times backsliding into bad habits. I would use the student observer to give me feedback about the usefulness of certain techniques (for example, the use of preview), but I would also have the observer help me more effectively to monitor the students' reactions so that I would better be able to get feedback during the semester.

References

Carroll, K.A. (1973). Observer in the classroom. *American Journal of Physics*, *41*, 1274-1282.

Casper, K.J. (1973). Use of observers in physics sections. *American Journal of Physics* , *41*, 1274-1282.

Helling, B.B. (1975). Looking for good teaching: A guide to peer observation. ERIC Document Reproduction Service - No. ED 186 380.

Laws, K. (1977). A classroom observer program. *Liberal Education* , *63*, 37-43.

Barbara Helling is the Coordinator of the St. Olaf Teaching Learning Center and and Associate Professor of Behavioral Science. Her academic background is in Educational Psychology and she has been in faculty development related activities since 1975. She may be contacted for more information about the program described in this chapter by writing to her at St. Olaf College, Northfield, MN 55057.

Diane Kuhlmann is an associate professor of accounting at St. Olaf College.

The Use of the Discussion Group for the Fine Tuning of Teaching

Richard G. Tiberius
Division of Studies in Medical Education
University of Toronto

Over the last decade I have developed a one-to-one consulting process designed specifically to elicit subtle feedback from students and to organize this feedback into a form which will be both understandable to teachers and useful in helping them to improve their teaching. The process is therefore particularly suited to what we may call "fine tuning," that is, helping experienced and capable teachers to reach even higher levels of excellence by improvements in such subtle areas as their relationships with students.

The central strategy in the consulting process described here is a method of gathering and reporting feedback. The process is therefore recommended for educational situations in which lack of feedback is the main problem. The process would probably not be very effective in helping teachers who are very well acquainted with their strengths and weaknesses but either lack the motivation to change, or do not know how to improve. In these latter two cases, strategies emphasizing reward systems or teaching skills might have a better chance of success compared to one emphasizing feedback. There are at least a dozen educational consultants using variations of this method across the continent. It seems to have been invented in different forms and used toward slightly different aims in each place.

The Process

Central Strategy

The central strategy involves the use of discussions between small groups of students lead by an experienced facilitator. Groups of six students are selected to ensure that, in the likely event of one or two absences, the group will still contain four or five members. Six is therefore regarded as a maximum and four a minimum. Three groups of students are chosen randomly from large classes (of fifty or more), two groups from medium size classes (of about ten to fifty), and just one group from classes of ten or fewer. My training in sampling statistics makes me uncomfortable about relying on only one group from a large class, but, in fact, my experience has been that two groups, randomly chosen from the same class, rarely differ in their opinions.

The assumptions underlying the use of this strategy are, first, that such discussion provides the kind of rich, descriptive information, filled out by colorful examples, which is necessary to communicate abstract, complex, or subtle feedback; and second, that the discussion process influences not only the kind of information but the form of the information. That is, the interaction between the students and the facilitator actually helps to organize the feedback into a coherent and understandable form. Although the process may also reveal rather obvious problems such as lettering on a transparency being too small, questionnaires are probably a more efficient means of communicating a problem such as small lettering to a teacher. The teacher will surely not ask, "In what sense are they too small? Can you give me some examples?" The process described below is designed to elicit examples and shades of meaning which appear to be necessary to the communication of more subtle issues about teaching.

Initial Meeting with Instructor

The first step is a meeting between the teacher and me (the consultant) at which time I attempt to find out three things: the teacher's objectives for the students, what he or she did to help the students achieve those objectives, and how he or she knew whether these objectives were fulfilled. The aim is for me to arrive at an understanding of the logic of the course from the teacher's point of view without frustrating him or her with a lot of educational jargon. The information provides a frame of reference for observation.

At this initial meeting, or even before it, the method of gathering information from students and of reporting it to the teacher is discussed with the teacher and the teacher's commitment to the process is secured. I ask the teacher to provide a class list from which I can randomly select the discussion groups, and a time table of the lectures so that I can arrange to visit one of them.

Group Discussion Session

As group facilitator I follow a rather strict procedure for leading these small group sessions with the students, although my style may appear casual. The purpose of this procedure is to eliminate, as far as possible, some of the inherent disadvantages of the free group discussion as a method of gathering evaluative feedback — such as dominance by a vocal minority or a tendency to force consensus that may narrow the range of opinion. I assure the students of the confidentiality of the discussion, I use a non-directive technique (especially during the first part of the session), ask clarifying questions, encourage each student to comment on each issue raised, assure students that the objective of the discussion is to achieve an understanding of the range of opinion, not to reach a consensus, and continually summarize their comments, repeating the summary for confirmation or correction by the group.

Preparation of the Written Report

Following the group session, I summarize the information collected under topic headings, prepare a written report several pages in length, and send it to the teacher.

Debriefing Meeting

After the teacher has had a chance to read the report, I meet with the teacher again for a discussion of its contents and his or her reaction to it. Particular attention is given to discrepancies between the teacher's conception of the goals, actions or evaluations of the course and the students' conception of those same components. Some suggestions for improvement are usually contributed by the students, and communicated to the teacher by means of the report, while other suggestions arise out of the discussion between the teacher and the consultant (me in this case). The teacher and I discuss the implementation of changes based on these suggestions.

Faculty Member's Response

Finally, it is desirable for the teacher to arrange to meet with the small group of students face-to-face, but only *after* he or she has assumed "ownership" of the issues. It is easier for teachers to lead such critical discussion groups when they are already familiar with the issues. Accepting criticism is difficult enough when one is prepared in advance.

The preceding description of the consulting process is the barest summary of a complex human interaction that rarely goes exactly as expected. In the real setting I am usually confronted by deviations from the standard pattern and by unforeseen problems. The consulting process therefore demands many little decisions along the way. The following case study is rather lengthy because I have attempted to interrupt the case with some of the most common of those unforeseen problems and my manner of handling them. I hope that you will find these interruptions more useful than distracting.

A Case Study

Making Contact

It was Professor Starr on the phone, reputed to be one of the best teachers of the Chemistry Department. I remembered his name from the teaching improvement workshop we had organized for his department the previous month. He told me that he was interested in the method demonstrated at the workshop, which he described as "the one that involved gathering feedback from students, observation of classes, and a written summary of the information for the teacher." Interestingly, his description left out two of the principle steps in the method: the interview with the teacher and the discussion of the report with the teacher for the purpose of generating suggestions for improvement. He appeared to be more interested in obtaining written documentation of a positive evaluation by his students than he was in engaging in the process of teaching improvement.

••• Not everyone calls the consultant for the right reasons, that is, to get help. Indeed, the best teachers are usually the first to come forward, ostensibly to seek improvement, but more out of an interest in documenting their competence, either for tenure and promotion or for personal satisfaction. However, working with these teachers should not be viewed as a waste of time. If they emerge from the process satisfied, the word will get around. Moreover, the ripple effect can be strengthened if you concentrate on a single department at a time. The alternative strategy, of initiating calls to problem teachers instead of waiting for them to contact me, could sour my relationship with them. Any initiative on my part raises their worst suspicions. It is better if they come to me.

There are other types of misinterpretation. For example, some teachers get the impression that the consulting process involves talking with them and visiting their classes but not interviewing their students. This viewpoint appears to be associated with teachers who feel threatened, and who seek an opportunity to convince someone that they are really not so bad but without risking exposure to their students. People hear what they want to hear.

I made an appointment to talk with Professor Starr about his teaching and asked him to send me a schedule of his classes so that I could visit one. He said that he taught two courses. "Which one would you like to visit?", he asked.

Without hesitation I answered "The one you are having trouble with, and the particular lecture that you are having the most trouble with, if that is possible."

••• This is my stock answer. It helps put teachers at ease by shifting their mind set from one of performing and covering their mistakes to one of disclosing their mistakes so that they can be detected and solved.

Starr was unable to decide which class I should visit since he felt that neither of them was really a problem. We decided on his lecture and lab course of 250 students. I asked him for a class list, broken down by lab section, so that I could draw the samples of students for the interviews from the labs instead of from the entire lecture group.

••• It is a lot easier to take a small random sample from a group of under twenty than from one of over a hundred. Besides, labs are a particularly easy place to meet students since there is often some free time near the end of the lab when I can talk to the group. In large classes, where I cannot see students directly after class, I have to make an appointment with them for a future date, taking my chances on their showing up, an especially risky procedure near exam time.

As soon as I hung up the phone I realized that I had forgotten to ask for his room number. Then, before I could call him back to get the number, my phone rang again. It was a professor from economics who was interested in the individualized consulting approach that she had heard about. I told her that I was concentrating on Chemistry this spring but that in the fall it would be possible to work with her, especially if I could work with several other professors from her department at the same time. I asked her to contact the staff development committee of her department so that we could arrange an introductory workshop of some kind. In my appointment book I marked down a potential involvement with economics for the fall. I would have agreed to consult with her if she had been in a desperate situation, however.

First Meeting with the Teacher

A week later Professor Starr and I had our meeting. A very dramatic fellow, he seemed to love teaching and wanted very much to get the rest of his faculty to enjoy it as much as he did and to do it as successfully. During our rather rambling conversation I asked him what his intentions were for the students, that is, what, in his view, the successful student should have learned as a result of his course. I also asked about what he did in and out of class to help students learn (planning the curriculum, writing handouts and so on). Finally, I asked how he knew whether his intentions for the students were realized. I was careful not to point out any similarity between my three questions and the educational cliche of "objectives, curriculum and evaluation." One should try not to bore.

I explained to him that my primary purpose for asking questions was to prepare myself for observation of his class. My observation time is much more productive if I know what the teacher is trying to accomplish. I added that sometimes, by discussing the components of a course, we can uncover inconsistencies between the components, or between students' views and teacher's views, and that such discrepancies are useful starting points for the improvement of teaching.

In-class Observation

I arrived early to his classroom in order to give myself an opportunity to observe and to listen to his students before the class began. I took a seat in the back row of the lecture hall so that I could observe the students as well as the teacher. Despite their large number, students quieted down as soon as he began to speak. His pauses, timing, voice, were excellent. There were so many things to observe and note. I took detailed notes: the key words he wrote on the overhead, the lighting, his handling of questions and of students arriving late, and so on. Yet despite my absorption in the task of observing his technique, and without very much prior interest in chemistry, I found myself wishing I were a student so that I could have asked a question at the question period. I left with a feeling that both chemistry and I were his dear friends, and that he was delighted to have the pleasure of introducing us.

Selecting the Students

The first lab group that I visited was in the middle of a rather time-consuming procedure which promised to take the entire period, according to the demonstrator, so I chose another one. In the second, students were just finishing up and were beginning to discuss the questions at the end of their lab notes. Since Professor Starr had forgotten to tell the demonstrator of my visit, as he had agreed to, there were some awkward minutes where I had to explain who I was and what I was doing in her lab. But I soon got the full cooperation of the demonstrator.

She asked the group if they would please give me their attention since I was there at the invitation of Professor Starr for the purpose of improving Chemistry 205. She introduced me warmly and sincerely, wishing me well in my attempt to improve the course. This kind of introduction is extremely helpful in establishing the students' trust in me. On another occasion, when I did not have such validation by the demonstrator, students saw me as the agent of the dean, spying on their teacher, and consequently told me very little.

The first thing I told the group was that I was _invited_ (an important word) to the class by Professor Starr because he was interested in improving the teaching of Chemistry 205. Then I explained that I chose to talk with students directly instead of using a questionnaire because I found that the information from discussions with students is so much richer, more elaborate, and provides us with a better picture of what to do in making useful changes. From questionnaires we can find out the answers to our own questions in our vocabulary. What we need to know is how the students themselves are thinking in their own vocabulary. I also made the point that the students in the sample would remain entirely anonymous and that they would be randomly chosen. At this point, as previously agreed, the demonstrator left the room for a few minutes so that the sample could be chosen without her knowing who the students were.

••• When there are no lab or tutorial sections attached to a lecture, or when the number of students in the lecture is small, I usually draw my random sample of students directly from the audience during a few minutes that the teacher reserves for me at the end. This procedure has the advantage of informing the entire class that there is an improvement process going on. It is important for students to have this information, because they are more likely to look with understanding on changes in the teacher's behavior if those changes are seen as part of a deliberate effort to improve his or her teaching.

••• The actual drawing of the sample is done rather dramatically. A class list which has been cut up into strips of paper, each containing an individual name of a student, is "tossed" like a salad, on the desk top. Then, while I look out at the students, away from the pile of names, I draw one name at a time and read it out, until I have six names. Each student, as his or her name is called, is asked to come to the front of the room. This is usually an occasion for general hooting and wisecracking. The more of this the better, since such group activity appears to invest the chosen students with a sense of obligation to represent their class. When I follow this procedure almost all of the students show up at the meeting as agreed.

Before I caught on to the importance of public commitment, I used to telephone the students, but the results were discouraging. After ten minutes of explaining to students who I was and what a random sample is and what I was trying to do, they would ask "Why me?" Then, after reluctantly agreeing to participate (some would ask me if they *had* to do it) they would frequently not show up for the meeting.

Since I did not have the student list in this particular case (Professor Starr said that he would send me one, but I should have reminded him knowing how busy he is) I simply referred to a table of random numbers, counting the students from left to right and raising my voice whenever a student number was selected by the random list. After choosing six, I told everyone in the lab that I would be talking with these six students, summarizing their opinions in a report, and discussing the report with their teacher in an attempt to improve his teaching. Finally, I made it clear that I was not trying to exclude anyone by this procedure, that I would take any information I could get from any other student who had anything to say, and that I was using the random method in order to get a sample that did not contain only complainers or only praisers.

As it happened, the students said that they would be finished with the lab early, so they would be able to meet me directly.

••• Usually, especially in the large lecture situation, I have to make an appointment for some future date. In the latter event, I try for a place familiar to the students, preferably close to a previous class, such as "the student lounge right opposite Econ 200." In this way, if one student forgets about the meeting, he or she may be reminded about it by seeing others going to it. Even so, I expect one or two drop-outs. By choosing six I have a little padding. Four is still enough for a discussion. Three cuts it close unless they are very interactive types. Two and one are really not acceptable numbers for what I am trying to do, as you will see.

The Discussion

The students suggested the cafeteria as a meeting place since it was uncrowded late in the afternoon. They clustered around me at one of the tables, waiting for me to ask questions, a natural enough assumption to make since I was there to find out information. I told them that although some questions did occur to me while I visited the class and while I talked with their professor, I was much more interested in finding out their thoughts about the course, in their own vocabulary, than in getting answers to my questions. If there was time at the end I might ask them some questions.

Since even this explanation did not convince them that I really did not intend to ask questions, I had to use another stock comment. I told them how the information would be used rather than telling them what kind of information I was looking for: "Please tell me anything you can which you think might be of use in improving the teaching of Chemistry 205. For example, you may want to comment on some aspect of the teaching which has been helpful for your learning and therefore should be maintained, or you may want to comment on some aspect of the teaching which has not been helpful and should be changed, and you may want to make suggestions as to how it should be changed." Then, by taking up my pen and writing a date on my pad, I signaled the students that I was prepared to take notes as they talked.

••• Because of the rule in polite conversation against arbitrarily changing the subject, there is a danger that the first topic raised will determine the subject of conversation for some time to come, resulting in other students forgetting the points that are uppermost in their minds. To overcome this problem I cut off other students from responding to the first comment by saying, while I wrote the comment down: "I would like to hear everyone's reaction to this point but, if we pause now to do that, some of you might forget the points that are uppermost on your minds and those are the very points that I do not want to miss. So let me go around quickly at first, jotting down all the major points, and then we'll return to them one at a time to get everyone's reaction to each point." Another way to overcome the problem of dominance by the first topic to be raised is to request every student to write down the main issues that he or she would like to raise, in brief phrases, before the discussion begins.

Comments flooded in. I briefly restated each one to make sure that I understood it properly. As we went back over them, eliciting everyone's reaction, a general discussion broke out over each point. I took notes quickly. At one point the group expressed discomfort over a dissenting view because they had assumed that I wanted a consensus. One student said: "I don't really agree that the lectures were useful but don't let me spoil the consensus." At this point I told the students that I was not looking for a consensus. I reminded them that since they were randomly chosen from over two hundred students, each minority view probably reflected the opinions of a sizable number of their classmates. "What I am interested in is the *range* of opinion rather than consensus," I told them, "Besides, since most teaching performances involve a trade off — if you do this you sacrifice that — I am interested in knowing why someone feels unhappy about something that others are happy about. I want to know all sides of the issue."

My goal was to end up with a number of paragraph length summaries of the issues that were critical to the success of Chemistry 205.

••• The facilitation process requires some group leadership skills such as the skill of encouraging students to react to each of the major points, summarizing comments, and repeating the summaries for

confirmation or correction. Rarely do I get the summary correct on
the first attempt. Moreover, corrections to my summary often
stimulate other comments resulting in a much more complete picture
of the issue.

Furthermore, the summaries should be as specific and as
descriptive as possible, to be useful to the teacher. Students' initial
comments often take the form of displays of emotion or vague
descriptions. There is no point in my telling a teacher that the
students are "put off" unless I also describe whether "put off" means
offended, bored or angered, and why they feel that way. One of the
most important tasks of the small group facilitator is to guide the
students from the emotional level of expression to the descriptive.

One student raised the issue of notes for the class, which
she described as "useless." Such a vague description was
typical of a first comment in that it was so devoid of meaning
that other students were not moved to comment on it. Not
until a second student asked what she had meant, and she had
offered the substitution "antiquated" for "useless" did a third
student offer a challenge: "But the articles were classics in the
field." After tossing this one back and forth for a while, it
became clear to everyone that a distinction needed to be made
between parts of the handouts — while the recommended
journal articles *were* useful, the syllabus notes badly needed
revision. Such a distinction would have undoubtedly evaded a
questionnaire which had asked students for a global rating of
the usefulness of the materials. We went on to another issue.

Finally, I encouraged the group to search for solutions,
not just problems. A number of suggestions for revision of
the syllabus came from the group, including some offers to
help.

There were only a few minutes before their next class
for me to check out some of my own hunches and to ask some
of the questions that Professor Starr had asked me to ask on
his behalf. I wanted to know why Starr had such high student
ratings. The students said because he was so stimulating. "He
really puts his heart into it, even though you don't learn very
much." "You can't take notes," another student said, "the
lectures aren't coherent enough, but they make you think."
Starr wanted to know whether the second lab was too long to
complete in the allowed two hours. Students said it was not.

Writing the Report

I returned to my office with about seven pages of notes thankful that I had the use of a word processor. Instead of having to organize all the material before writing the report, I could type out the quotes from students just as they appeared in my notes, rearranging them into appropriate sections as I went along. (There were times when I wished that I had read the book that I had borrowed on speed writing.) Although the report consists of a series of brief summaries explaining student views, whenever possible I added supporting quotations to each summary. The quotations, cited verbatim from the students, gave color and life to the report.

The report was five pages long. I pondered whether to give Professor Starr a copy to read over before discussing it with him or to discuss it first and then write the report. I always anguish over this decision. The former method is sure to get his attention. The latter will produce a more balanced and accurate report because it will be modified by my sensitivity to his reaction. I chose the former in this case. Starr is going to need something to get his attention. He is expecting nothing more than a confirmation of his excellent reputation.

Debriefing Meeting

There were enough positive comments in the report to support Professor Starr in his style of lecturing. Specifically, there was sufficient confirmation of his belief in enthusiasm and caring as important dimensions of teaching. He deserved his reputation. On the other hand, there were some surprises for him. Despite their enjoyment of the lectures, students expressed their anxiety in facing the exam without a coherent set of notes. What they needed was some definition of "core" material for the course. Starr's lectures failed to provide that. The syllabus was no help. And, although some of the other lecturers in the course were more organized, incoherency between various lecturers in the course made it extremely difficult for students to discern the level of detail that was expected.

It was interesting to me that although the definition of "core" material was the students' main concern, it was not even present in my own notes, based on my visit to the class and my discussion with Professor Starr. Obviously, my notes were no substitute for student comments. However, the fact that my own notes raised different issues from those raised by the students did not invalidate my perceptions. On the contrary, I was confident that my notes would be useful because they would bring out aspects of the teaching that students were not aware of while they were busy attending to the content. The students and I have different perspectives: they have to pass the exam, while I can view the lecture more as theatre.

The teacher has a third perspective — ego involvement in the success of the teaching. Starr defended himself. He said that he had always believed the proper role of a lecturer lay in stimulation of students, not in providing information. I agreed that he had been stimulating, and I agreed with the appropriateness of "stimulation" as an objective for a lecture. I did not draw attention to the fact that he was defending himself and certainly did not try to counter his defense. I consider it a serious mistake for the consultant to counter the teacher's defense with a series of "Yes, but" rejoinders, although it is tempting to do so because the defensive teacher appears to misunderstand or not accept the point.

The teacher is usually painfully aware of the strength of the criticism, so much so that his or her own position may seem irrational. Since it is reprehensible to act without reason in our culture, the teacher must give a rationale, a defense, for why he or she has not, for example, provided students with an organization of the material. In my response to Starr, I attempted to recognize and to validate his defense. Then I waited. I just kept quiet for a little bit, and predictably, he said: "But my point about stimulation really doesn't solve the students' problem of needing some outline of the material, does it? Maybe I could give them the page numbers of material to read, or sample questions, or rewrite that handout. You know, the handout is really not very well done as far as its major objective of giving the students some direction for their study."

This is the point at which input from me could be useful, *after* the teacher has engaged the problem himself. I said: "If you do improve the handouts it may also be useful to let the students know what you consider to be the main function of your handouts and of your lecture. In that way they won't have false expectations for either." We compared the feedback from the students with my observations, and we set both against the background of Starr's own objectives and methods. These comparisons stimulated a very productive discussion. Not only did suggestions arise that might improve his teaching effectiveness, but the objectives of the lectures were reconsidered in the light of student objectives and of the stated aims of the course. This constructive dialogue with Starr followed naturally, without prompting from me, as soon as the feedback had been accepted and understood. But had I not accepted his defense, he may have blocked out or rejected the feedback, and the creative phase that followed may have been replaced by an unproductive exchange of accusations and counter accusations.

Follow Up

Sometimes, this discussion is the last I see of a teacher. It is sad when I cannot see the results of my work. Fortunately, in the case of Professor Starr, the situation was very different. He wanted me to repeat the process during the second semester. In the interim he said he would speak with students himself, discussing some of the changes that we had suggested and asking them what they might suggest to overcome the shortcomings of the course.

This action was somewhat of a breakthrough for Professor Starr, as he told me much later. Despite all his good rapport with students, he had never talked to them directly about teaching. He enjoyed teaching and feared losing his motivation through harsh criticism. But he found the discussions less threatening than he expected, when, as he said, it was he who initiated the criticisms. Somehow it gave him a sense of control and confidence to be able to approach the students with a list of "his" criticisms although, ultimately, they had come from the students, and ask for their advice.

Advantages and Disadvantages of the Process

Although names and courses have been changed, this is a true story, one which has been repeated with minor variations, since then. According to students, the teacher, and this consultant, the course has been enormously improved. There is no question in my mind that the process can be effective in bringing about changes in teacher behaviors or teaching programs which are seen as improvements by everyone concerned. The main drawback is that it is very time-consuming for the consultant. The total investment on the part of the consultant is approximately eight hours from the initial interview through writing of the report to the final interview. My colleagues and I are currently experimenting with information gathering techniques which maintain the benefits of group interaction while reducing the consultant time.

References

Cammann, C. (1982). Feedback systems for teachers. In James Bess (Ed.), *Motivating professors to teach effectively* (pp. 85-94). San Francisco: Jossey-Bass.

Clark, D.J. & Bekey, J. (1979). Use of small groups in instructional evaluation. *Professional and Organizational Development Quarterly*, *1*, 2, 87-95.

Lomax, P. & McLeman, P. (1984). The uses and abuses of nominal group technique in polytechnic course evaluation. *Studies in Higher Education*, *9*, 2, 183-190.

Tiberius, R. (1984). Individualized consulting to improve teaching. *To Improve the Academy*, *3*, 119-127. (Pittsburgh, PA: Duff's Business Institute)

Richard G. Tiberius is an Associate Professor in the Division of Studies in Medical Education & Family & Community at the University of Toronto. He pioneered the consultation technique described in this paper and is engaged in service and research to improve the teaching of the Faculty of Medicine. For more information, he can be reached at: Room 83D, FitzGerald Bldg., 150 College Street, Toronto, Ontario, CANADA M5S 1A8 , (416) 978-2124.

Using an Objective Observation System to Diagnose Teaching Problems

Karron G. Lewis
Center for Teaching Effectiveness
The University of Texas at Austin

At the Center for Teaching Effectiveness (CTE) one-to-one consultation is probably the most effective method we have to instill long-term changes in the teaching techniques of individual faculty members. The CTE staff members have been trained in objective observation techniques and are skilled in the analysis of teacher-student interactions which take place during a class session. They are also skilled in the analysis of course materials and typically provide feedback to each instructor concerning the effectiveness of the handouts, exams, and so forth, used in the course.

The Consultation Process

Pre-Observation Conference

A pre-observation conference is scheduled when we are first contacted by a faculty member . The faculty member is asked to bring texts, their current syllabus, past exams, and the like to help the consultant get an idea of the content and cognitive level of the course. Copies of past student evaluations are also requested to provide some idea of how the students have felt about the course and instructor in the past. During the pre-observation conference the consultant and faculty member discuss the concerns and questions which made the faculty member seek assistance. This is also a time for the consultant to get to know the faculty member and vice versa. At the end of this conference, the consultant and faculty member will decide on a time for the in-class observations to occur.

In-Class Observations

Normally three in-class observations are made before the consultant will discuss these observations with the faculty member. This procedure allows the consultant to make sure the observations were representative of the normal teaching process (that is, only one observation might fall on a "bad" day).

During the first observation the consultant typically takes notes as if he or she were a student to determine the pace of the lecture, the organization and clarity of the material presented, and so forth. A general observation form is also filled out during this class session (see **Figure 1**) to provide information about the faculty member's teaching style, the type of classroom, and the attentiveness and characteristics of the students.

Using the Cognitive Interaction Analysis System (CIAS)

Coding the verbal interactions. During the second and third observations the consultant codes the verbal interactions which take place using the *Cognitive Interaction Analysis System* (CIAS).[1] The categories for this system are shown in **Figure 2.** In using this system, one category is recorded every three seconds or whenever a change in the interaction occurs, whichever comes first. Thus, each block of codes on the coding sheet (see sample Coding Sheet in **Figure 3**)

---

[1] The basic ten categories for this system were developed by Glenn Ross Johnson at Texas A&M University. The subcategories were added by the Center staff at The University of Texas at Austin to provide greater depth and more specificity to our descriptions of what happened in the classroom. Though they were originally added for a research study, our staff has continued to use them because we have found that faculty members appreciate the added detail.

Center for Teaching Effectiveness
Classroom Observation Form

Instructor_____ Observer_____ Date_____

1. THE COURSE: Number:_____Title:_____
   Meeting time:_____

2. LEVEL: ___Freshman ___Sophomore ___Junior ___Senior
   ___Graduate

3. CLASS: No. Students:_____ Description of room:_____
   _____Where students sit:_____

4. SUBJECT FOR THE HOUR:_____

5. METHOD:

6. THE INSTRUCTOR:

   Speaking style:

   Use of Movement/Gestures:

   Use of Media:

   Enthusiasm:

   Handouts:

7. THE STUDENTS:

   Attentiveness (beginning vs. end):

   Questions:

   Evidence of Understanding:

   Notetaking:

8. GENERAL COMMENTS:

Figure 1. Observation Form for First Classroom Visit

Expanded CIAS Categories

1 - Accepting Student Attitudes
   1h - Use of Humor
   1f - Affective Instructor
       Comments
2 - Positive Reinforcement

3 - Repeating a Student Response
   3f - Giving Corrective Feedback
   3b - Building on a Student
       Response

4 - Asking Questions
   4c - Knowledge/Comprehension
       Level
   4e - Application (Example) Level
   4a - Analysis Level
   4y - Synthesis Level
   4j - Evaluation (Judgement)
       Level
   4f - Affective Questions
   4s - Process or Structure
       Questions
   4r - Rhetorical Questions
   4p - Probing Questions

5 - Lecturing
   5v - Simultaneous Visual &
       Verbal Presentation
   5e - Using Examples/Analogies
   5r - Reviewing
   5x - Answering a Student
       Question
   5m - Mumbling
   5t - Reading Verbatim from
     Text/Overhead/Board/Slide

6 - Providing Cues
   6m - Focusing on Main Points
   6d - Giving Directions
   6c - Calling on a Student
   6s - Giving
       Assignments/Process
   6v - Cues with Visual
       Presentation

7 - Criticism of Student Answer/
    Behavior

8 - Cognitive Student Talk
   8c-8j - Answers to Teacher
       Questions
   8n - Student Doesn't Know
       Answer
   8q - Student Question

   8h - Student Laughter
   8g - Students Working in
       Groups
   8i - Students Working
       Individually

9 - Non-cognitive Student Talk

0 - Silence
   0b - Writing on Board/
       Overhead w/o Talking
   0m - Mumbling (a general
       low roar)
   0l - Listening/Watching

Figure 2. Expanded CIAS Categories.

IA Observation Form
Center for Teaching Effectiveness

Instructor:_____   Date:_____   Class:_____
No. Students: 22

Time: 9:04 Topic: Handing papers | Time: 9:12 Topic: Going over assgn.

0	4s	4s	0	4s		5	5r	5	5	5
6s	4s	4s	4s	4s		5	5r	5	5	6m
6s	0m	4s	4s	4s		5	5	5	5	6m
0m	0m	4s	8s	0m		5	5	5	5	5
6s	4s	4s	0	0m		5	5	5	5	5
4s	4s	0m	4s	4s		5	5	5	5	5r
0m	4s	4s	4s	4s		5	5	5	5	5r
4s	4s	0m	4s	2f		5r	5	5	5	5r

Time: 9:06 Topic: (same) | Time: 9:14 Topic: Prob. w/original

4s	4s	0m	6	6		5	5	5	6d	5
4s	4s	6s	6	6		5	5	5	5	5
4s	0m	6s	0m	6		5	5	5	5	5
4s	0m	6	7	6		5	5	5	5	5
4s	8	6	7	0		5	5	5	5	5
0m	4s	6	7	0		5	5	4r	5t	5
0m	8	6	6	6		5	5	4r	5t	5
4s	4s	6	6	0		5	5	5	5t	5

Time: 9:09 Topic: giving hndouts | Time: 9:16 Topic: (same)

0	6s	0	6s	5t		5	5	5v	5	5
0	6s	5	5t	5		5	5	5v	5	5
0	6s	5	5t	5		5	5	5v	4s	5
0	6s	5	5t	5		5	5	5v	4s	5
0	6	5	5t	5		5	5	5	5	5
6d	0	5	5t	5		5	5v	5	5	5
0	0	5	5t	5		5	5v	5	5	5
0	0	6s	5t	5		5	5v	5	5	5

Comments: Really could ask more questions. Students seem like they would enjoy participating more. Examples of the types of communication being discussed would help students understand the nuances of the forms.

Figure 3. Sample CIAS coding sheet.

Directions: Each sequence of CIAS codes is read from the top of the column to the bottom. The comment section interprets the interaction pattern which is represented by the codes to the left of it.

Sequence	Comment
6s 6s 6d 6d 6 6c 8q	This sequence indicates that the instructor began by giving the students an assignment (6s) or indicated a procedure which they should follow in completing an assignment. Directions for completing this process were then given (6d). The instructor then told the students what they were going to be covering that day in the lecture (6). This is followed by the instructor calling on a student (6c) who then asks a question (8q).
4a 4a 0 0 8a	In this sequence, the instructor asks a question which would be classified as being at the Analysis level (4a). The question is then followed by six seconds of silence, or "think time" (0), and finally, the question is answered by a student (8a).
8q 8q 5x 5x	When the students ask a question, it is recorded as 8q. The instructor's answer to that question is recorded as 5x. This provides information as to whether the instructor is spending adequate time or too much time in answering each student's question.
4e 4e 8e 8e 8e 2 3 3b	This sequence shows that the instructor asked a question at the Application level (4e) and it was answered by a student (8e). It took the student nine seconds to answer the question. This is typical for a higher level question. The instructor then praised the student's answer (that is, "That's right, Joe."),repeated the student's answer so the rest of the class could hear it, and then used the student's answer to explain the concept further (3b).

Figure 4. Some typical CIAS category sequences and their explanations.

represents approximately two minutes of class time. When reading or analyzing these codes you read down each column of numbers in each "block" and then go to the block below it; as illustrated by the arrows on the sample coding sheet. These codes can then tell us the sequence of verbal interactions which took place during the class session. Several typical category sequences are described in **Figure 4**.

Putting the data in a matrix. After the observation data have been collected, the numerals recorded are paired (as illustrated in **Figure 5**) and recorded in a 16 x 16 matrix. (Since it would be *very* difficult to create and analyze a 49 x 49 matrix, the categories are collapsed back into the original ten categories plus six additional categories which tend to effect classroom climate.) The first numeral of each pair of numbers (codes) designates the row while the second numeral of the same pair designates the column. A tally for a pair appears on the matrix where that row and column intersect; for example, a tally in the 3-6 cell means a 3 was followed by a 6 — see **Figure 6**. The last numeral of the previous pair is then combined with the next numeral to form the next pair. After entering tallies for all of the number pairs, the number of tallies in each cell of the matrix indicate how many times that particular interaction sequence occurred during the observation. For example, if you have 15 tallies in the 4-8 cell, that tells you that there were 15 times when the instructor asked a question and a student answered immediately — with no silent "think or wait time" in between.

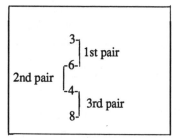

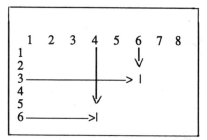

Figure 5 - Pairing #s for entry into matrix.

Figure 6 - Tallies entered in matrix cells.

If this sounds like way too much trouble, it is! — *if* you do it by hand. Luckily, we have a computer program (currently for the Apple II+) in which you only have to enter the numbers as you see them on your coding form; they do not have to be paired and the computer prints out a matrix like that shown in **Figure 7**. (A programed workbook — which contains a listing of this computer program — and audio cassette skill training tape are available for purchase. Details are given at the end of this chapter.)

Analysis of data in the matrix. It is recommended that you use a clockwise flow when analyzing the actual data appearing in the cells of the matrix. To find a pattern where an instructor asks a question, the student responds to the question, and the teacher provides positive reinforcement, one would look across row four (4) to its intersection with column eight (8) — in Figure 6 the number in this cell is 12. This number tells us that a student immediately responded to twelve of the instructor's questions. Moving down column eight (8) to the intersection of row eight (8), we find that the students' answers frequently lasted more than three seconds — there are 36 tallies in cell 8-8. This is often an indication that the questions being asked were at higher cognitive levels. Now look across row eight to the left until you reach column two (2). The number in this cell (8-2) tells us that the instructor positively reinforced seven (7) of the students' answers.

Another key cell is the 4-10 cell which indicates how many times the instructor left "wait-time" after asking a question to give the students time to think of an answer. If this number is quite a bit lower than the 4-8 cell then look at the 4-5 cell to determine whether the instructor is inclined to answer his or her own questions. Though the instructor in the sample matrix frequently left "wait-time" (4-10 cell), it was usually followed by another question (10-4 cell), an explanation (10-5 cell) or a direction or cue (10-6 cell). Only once was the "wait-time" followed by a student answer (10-8 cell).

The first row of numbers at the bottom of the matrix indicate how many "tallies" were in each column. The row below that indicates the percent of the total tallies which that represents (that is, the percent of class time the instructor and students spent in that type of interaction).

INTERACTION ANALYSIS

	1	2	3	4	5	6	7	8	9	10	11	12	13	14	15	16
1/	0	0	0	0	0	0	0	0	0	0	0	0	0	0	0	0
2/	0	4	4	2	9	0	0	2	0	0	0	0	0	0	0	0
3/	0	2	7	2	2	0	0	1	0	0	0	0	0	0	0	0
4/	0	1	0	35	8	0	1	12	0	10	0	0	9	0	0	0
5/	0	6	0	18	767	23	1	0	0	3	0	1	1	6	0	0
6/	0	0	0	3	17	56	0	0	0	12	0	0	0	1	0	0
7/	0	0	0	0	1	1	3	1	0	0	0	0	0	0	0	0
8/	0	7	3	3	3	0	0	36	0	1	0	0	0	0	0	0
9/	0	0	0	0	0	0	0	0	0	0	0	0	0	0	0	0
10/	0	0	0	2	7	2	1	1	0	32	0	0	0	0	0	0
11/	0	0	0	0	0	0	0	0	0	0	0	0	0	0	0	0
12/	0	0	0	0	3	0	0	0	0	0	0	11	0	1	0	0
13/	0	1	0	3	6	0	0	0	0	0	0	0	8	0	0	0
14/	0	0	0	1	3	0	0	0	0	1	0	3	0	25	0	0
15/	0	0	0	0	0	0	0	0	0	0	0	0	0	0	0	0
16/	0	0	0	0	0	0	0	0	0	0	0	0	0	0	0	0
sum	0	21	14	76	826	89	6	53	0	59	0	15	18	33	0	0
%	0	1.7	1.2	6.3	68.3	7.4	.5	4.4	0	4.9	0	1.2	1.5	2.7	0	0

```
************************
TOTAL ENTRIES:  1210
% TT:           86.529
% ST:            5.868
% PSSR:         61.972
% TSSR:         84.336
% ID:             .106
************************
```

Matrix Categories

1 - Accepting student attitudes
2 - Positive reinforcement
3 - Repeating student response
4 - Questions
5 - Lecture
6 - Cues/directions
7 - Criticism
8 - Cognitive student talk

9 - Non-cognitive student talk
10 - Silence
11 - Humor (1h)
12 - Visual & verbal presentation (5v)
13 - Student questions (8q)
14 - Writing on board w/o talking (0b)
15 - Students working in groups (8g)
16 - Students working individually (8i)

Figure 7. Sample CIAS matrix.

Below the matrix is a small table which shows the total number of codes which were recorded (TOTAL ENTRIES), the percentage of time the instructor spent talking (%TT), the percentage of time the students spent talking and/or participating (%ST), the percentage of time the students spent in extended talk (i.e., the 8-8, 9-9, 13-13, 15-15, and 16-16 cells) (%PSSR), the percentage of time the instructor spent in extended talk (i.e., in the 1-1, 2-2, 3-3, 4-4, 5-5, 6-6, 7-7, 11-11, and 12-12 cells) (%TSSR), and the indirect/direct ratio (%ID) which indicates whether the classroom atmosphere was more direct (less than .5) or indirect (.5 and above).

Preparation of data for client and post-observation consultation. Utilizing all of the written course materials and in-class observation information, the consultant then writes out a *detailed description* of what was observed along with an analysis of the probable sources for the concerns expressed in the pre-observation conference. Then another conference session is scheduled in which the consultant shares with the faculty member the information which was gathered during the in-class observations.

At the beginning of this post-observation consultation session the faculty member is asked to describe his or her objectives for each of the observed classes and whether or not those objectives were met. If there were objectives which were not met, the faculty member is asked to generate ideas for techniques which might have been used to meet those objectives. After the consultant has obtained this information concerning how the faculty member felt the classes went then they move on to an analysis and discussion of the data which was collected.

The first step in the data analysis portion of the consultation session is to give the faculty member a copy of the notes which were taken during the first observation. These are discussed and analyzed for organization and content. During the observations, the consultant may also make marginal notes which elaborate on things like the pace of the lecture, the attentiveness of the students, the instructor's utilization of media and so forth. These are also discussed and the faculty member and consultant brainstorm possible solutions to any problems which were noted.

Next, a handout is given to the faculty member which lists the CIAS codes and explains the coding process. These are discussed until the consultant is sure that the faculty member understands the process and then copies of the actual data sheets are presented. Typical interaction sequences are pointed out by the consultant and the faculty member is encouraged to ask questions and hypothesize what might have happened if a different sequence had taken place.

The data analysis usually points out interaction techniques which could be improved or changed to facilitate student participation and possible changes are discussed. For example, if all the questions which are asked are followed by lecture rather than by student responses, the instructor usually says something like, "I've been wondering why the students don't answer my questions, now I know. I answer all of them myself!"

Together the consultant and faculty member will decide how to facilitate any changes the faculty member may wish to make in his or her teaching and training sessions for the development of more complex teaching skills may be scheduled. If the faculty member feels the changes can be made without these training sessions, then methods for accomplishing these changes are discussed and a follow-up observation time is scheduled (typically three or four weeks later).

Follow-up observation. During the follow-up observation the consultant will focus on the skills and techniques identified for possible change or improvement. Usually the verbal interactions are coded again, analyzed, and discussed with the faculty member. Another detailed memorandum is written and a decision is made as to whether the process should continue.

The sequence of events outlined above can occur as many times as needed until the faculty member is satisfied with his or her teaching. (Sometimes only one or two sessions are required and sometimes an extended period of assistance is requested — for example, several semesters.)

Faculty reactions to CIAS. Because the primary tool used in this process is an objective observation system, it provides some convincing "hard data" to illustrate some possible causes for particular problems. The first reaction of most faculty members to this tool is amazement. Then, after the significance of the data is explained to them, they become excited about the information it can provide. The most notable change, which is usually seen immediately, is a heightened awareness of the students and their role in the learning process. Interaction is now encouraged and often the faculty member expresses a desire to learn how to question at higher cognitive levels.

CIAS can also be used with videotaped class segments. The videotape provides conclusive evidence that "there was no silence after that question so the students didn't have an opportunity to think of an answer." The videotaped class session also enables the client to follow along on the coded sheet for a better understanding of just what the codes represent.

In the eight years during which this consultation process has been used, there have only been one or two faculty members who reacted negatively to the "hard data." They seemed to feel this process was too detailed and they had trouble understanding how changing minute interactions could help their teaching. Usually, however, using this system in connection with the consultation process provides more concrete data which are appreciated by our research-oriented clientele.

A Case Study

Around the middle of July, Dr. Dollar called and indicated that he was not very happy with the Course/Instructor Survey (CIS) results he had just received for his Spring classes. He felt that they were very low and said he would like for me to look at them and possibly suggest some things he could do to bring them up. I made an appointment for him to come to my office the next day and asked him to bring his evaluations, a syllabus, his text, handouts, copies of his exams and anything else he used to teach his class.

Pre-Observation Conference

The next day when Dr. Dollar and I met, I discovered that he was teaching two sections of a required course in

Business Finance with 150 students in each section. Two strikes against him already!! And, his evaluation averages *were* quite low. (On a five-point scale which goes from +2.0 to -2.0, most of his averages were between -.5 and +.5; most good instructors' averages are +1.0 and above.) The written comments on his evaluations indicated that the students felt he was too busy to be bothered by them outside of class and that he was not very approachable. I was somewhat surprised at this because he was very personable and easy to talk to during our meeting. He indicated, however, that he was *very protective* of his research time and said he did *not* encourage students to come in "just to chat."

His syllabus was very organized and it was evident that he had given a lot of thought to the way in which he was teaching the course. There were ample opportunities for the students to practice what they were learning *and* to obtain feedback on their progress through weekly quizzes and required homework problems. In addition, there were two mid-semester exams and a comprehensive final exam.

Since Dr. Dollar's major problem seemed to be the way he related to the students, we discussed things he could do to improve rapport without taking up extra time outside of class. Because he didn't want a line of students outside his office during his office hours, I suggested that he schedule "Help Sessions" instead of one-to-one office hours. This way he could interact with a smaller number of students at a time and answer questions only once or twice instead of 20 or 30 times! Effective use of the time before and after class could also help him get to know the students and answer a number of "immediate" questions. Much of the research on teaching large classes indicates that the students feel very isolated because they don't know anyone else in the class. So, I suggested that it might help if he have the students form study groups with three or four students in each group. These groups could be encouraged to work together on homework assignments and possibly during some in-class problem solving sessions. Then, I made arrangements to observe his class on the first day to see if I could pick up any verbal or non-verbal messages he might be transmitting to the students; an aloof demeanor, lack of eye contact, and so forth.

First Observation

During my first-day observation, the first thing I noticed was that Dr. Dollar was a little late for class; his Teaching Assistant came in first and set things up. (This gave the impression that Dr. Dollar, himself, was too good for things like setting up the overhead projector.) Next, the lights were *very low* — so low that it was almost impossible to read one's notes. From the middle of the room I had trouble distinguishing Dr. Dollar's facial features. (When I mentioned this problem after class he said it was so the students could see the overheads better. I told him that I was having trouble seeing well enough to write and suggested he try it with the lights up next time and ask the students which they preferred. I also reminded him that in order to build rapport, he needed to arrive a little early and stay after class a while.) On the positive side, however, because there were fewer students than chairs, he did ask the students to sit toward the front of the class and told them he wouldn't be using the mike because he always choked himself on the cord. (A little humor!) Most of the students seemed to think that this was a reasonable request and they moved into the first eight rows.

Second Observation

I was glad to see Dr. Dollar in the classroom when I arrived around five minutes before the class was to start. Evidently the students were glad to see him too because a number of them were talking to him. I also noted that the lights were up and the overhead transparency image could be seen quite clearly from the back of the room. This latter change made the class atmosphere seem *much* more open and made Dr. Dollar appear more receptive to student input.

During this observation I coded the verbal interactions using the Expanded CIAS and a number of significant patterns emerged upon analysis of the data (See **Figure 8**):

1. First, Dr. Dollar talked 92.4% of the class time (51 minutes) and the students participated during 5.0% of the class time (2.8 minutes). The class lasted a total of 55

INTERACTION ANALYSIS

	1	2	3	4	5	6	7	8	9	10	11	12	13	14	15*	16*
1/	**15**	0	0	1	1	1	0	0	0	2	0	0	0	0	0	0
2/	0	3	6	5	9	2	0	3	0	0	1	2	2	0	0	0
3/	0	2	6	10	16	1	0	1	0	0	1	6	0	0	0	0
4/	1	1	1	7	**26**	3	0	42	0	**3**	1	2	18	0	0	0
5/	1	2	0	39	408	20	1	7	0	11	7	18	10	0	0	0
6/	1	1	0	8	13	65	0	0	0	6	0	7	3	0	0	0
7/	0	0	0	0	0	1	0	0	0	0	0	0	0	0	0	0
8/	1	**12**	27	8	11	2	0	14	0	0	5	2	1	0	0	0
9/	0	0	0	0	0	0	0	0	0	0	0	0	0	0	0	0
10/	0	0	0	5	4	5	0	1	0	64	0	5	7	0	0	0
11/	0	0	0	0	1	0	0	13	0	1	13	0	0	0	0	0
12/	1	1	0	17	13	4	0	2	0	3	0	96	1	0	0	0
13/	0	11	2	5	22	0	0	1	0	1	0	0	28	0	0	0
14/	0	0	0	0	0	0	0	0	0	0	0	0	0	0	0	0
15/	0	0	0	0	0	0	0	0	0	0	0	0	0	0	0	0
16/	0	0	0	0	0	0	0	0	0	0	0	0	0	0	0	0
sum	20	33	42	105	524	104	1	84	0	91	28	138	70	0	0	0
%	1.6	2.7	3.4	8.5	42.3	8.4	.1	6.8	0	7.3	2.3	11.1	5.6	0	0	0

****

TOTAL ENTRIES: 1240 (~62 min.)
%TT: 80.24
%ST: 12.42
%PSSR:27.27
%TSSR:61.61
%ID: .23
****

Matrix Categories

1 - Accepting student attitudes
2 - Positive reinforcement
3 - Repeating student response
4 - Questions
5 - Lecture
6 - Cues/directions
7 - Criticism
8 - Cognitive student talk

9 - Non-cognitive student talk
10 - Silence
11 - Humor (1h)
12 - Visual & verbal presentation (5v)
13 - Student questions (8q)
14 - Writing on board w/o talking (0b)
15 - Students working in groups (8g)
16 - Students working individually (8i)

(NOTE: Categories 15 and 16 were added after this class was observed.)

Figure 8.   Case study observation matrix #1.

minutes. The first 30 minutes of the class consisted of a "Refresher" on the concepts and skills the students were expected to have if they planned to do well in the course and during the next 30 minutes he began discussing new content.

2. Dr. Dollar asked 72 questions in the course of the class session. The types of questions and when they occurred during the class are listed below:

Question Type	Total	Review	New Mat.
4c-Know/Comp	18	17	1
4e-Application	17	10	7
4a-Analysis	4	3	1
4j-Evaluation	1	0	1
4f-Affective	1	1	0
4s-Process	2	2	0
4r-Rhetorical	25	8	17
4p-Probing	4	3	1
TOTAL	72	41	31

Thus, we found that he tended to use Rhetorical questions (4r) when presenting new material and asked Knowledge/Comprehension (4c) and Application (4e) questions during the review. I also noted that he left no "wait-time" after asking a question and if the students didn't answer right away, he answered the question himself. (There was only one tally in the 4-10 cell on the matrix and twenty-six tallies in the 4-5 cell.)

3. The generous use of the 5e (Giving examples) category on the data sheets indicated that Dr. Dollar provided numerous examples for the concepts which were being presented.

4. The 6m (Cueing main points) code occurred fairly often which indicated that Dr. Dollar was emphasizing main points and frequently wrote them on the overhead transparency, as indicated by numerous 6m-5v sequences.

5. The frequent occurrence of the 5m (Mumbling) code indicated that Dr. Dollar needed to maintain breath support, especially at the ends of his sentences, so his voice would be audible.

Because Dr. Dollar seemed to be taking my suggestions to heart, I decided that it would be best to give him some immediate feedback about ways to encourage more student interaction so, I spoke with him briefly after class. I encouraged him to try to ask even more questions which would get the students involved and also to provide opportunities for the students to do some actual problem-solving during class (i.e., work with their study group or with the student sitting next to them to solve a problem and then share their solutions). I also suggested that he needed to maintain the volume of his voice toward the end of his sentences.

Third Observation

I coded the interaction during this class session and there were some significant changes (see **Figure 9**):

1. The %TT went down to 80.2% (49.7 minutes) and the %ST went up to 12.4% (8 minutes)! This class session lasted a total of 62 minutes. Dr. Dollar was using the student-group problem solving activities which I had suggested previously. He gave the students approximately 10 minutes to work the problem in their groups; spent the next 20 minutes going over the problem; spent the next 20 minutes discussing and elaborating on material the students had read in their text; and spent the last 20 minutes presenting new material.

2. Dr. Dollar asked 98 questions. Below they are categorized by type and when they occurred in the class session:

INTERACTION ANALYSIS

	1	2	3	4	5	6	7	8	9	10	11	12	13	14	15*	16*
1/	3	0	0	1	0	1	0	0	0	0	1	0	0	0	0	0
2/	0	2	9	0	4	0	0	0	0	2	0	0	0	0	0	0
3/	0	3	25	5	19	0	0	0	0	1	1	3	0	0	0	0
4/	1	0	0	13	26	3	0	33	0	1	0	5	4	0	0	0
5/	1	2	0	44	466	31	0	1	0	5	3	18	5	0	0	0
6/	0	0	0	2	23	85	0	0	0	3	2	11	0	0	0	0
7/	0	0	0	0	0	0	0	0	0	0	0	0	0	0	0	0
8/	0	8	19	2	8	0	0	2	0	0	0	1	0	0	0	0
9/	0	0	0	0	0	0	0	0	0	0	0	0	0	0	0	0
10/	0	0	0	1	8	3	0	0	0	9	0	6	0	0	0	0
11/	0	0	0	1	4	0	0	3	0	0	2	0	0	0	0	0
12/	1	0	0	16	14	2	0	1	0	6	1	98	1	2	0	0
13/	0	2	4	0	4	0	0	0	0	0	0	0	5	0	0	0
14/	0	0	0	1	0	1	0	0	0	0	0	0	0	0	0	0
15/	0	0	0	0	0	0	0	0	0	0	0	0	0	0	0	0
16/	0	0	0	0	0	0	0	0	0	0	0	0	0	0	0	0
sum	6	17	57	86	576	126	0	40	0	27	10	142	15	2	0	0
%	0	1.5	5.2	7.8	52.2	11.4	0	3.6	0	2.4	.9	12.9	1.4	.2	0	0

****

TOTAL ENTRIES: 1104 (~55 min.)
%TT: 92.39
%ST: 4.98
%PSSR:12.73
%TSSR:68.04
%ID: .17

****

Matrix Categories

1 -	Accepting student attitudes		9 -	Non-cognitive student talk
2 -	Positive reinforcement		10 -	Silence
3 -	Repeating student response		11 -	Humor (1h)
4 -	Questions		12 -	Visual & verbal presentation (5v)
5 -	Lecture		13 -	Student questions (8q)
6 -	Cues/directions		14 -	Writing on board w/o talking (0b)
7 -	Criticism		15 -	Students working in groups (8g)
8 -	Cognitive student talk		16 -	Students working individually (8i)

(NOTE: Categories 15 and 16 were added after this class was observed.)

Figure 9.   Case study observation matrix #2.

Type Question	Total	Work Prob.	Disc. Prob.	Disc.	New
4c-Know/Comp	19	0	5	10	4
4e-Application	20	0	6	14	0
4a-Analysis	10	0	1	2	6
4j-Evaluation	1	0	0	1	0
4s-Process	11	3	3	3	2
4r-Rhetorical	14	0	3	6	5
4p-Probing	12	1	1	8	2
TOTAL	98	4	21	51	22
8q-St. Quest.	42	13	10	12	7

The number of student questions asked are also listed above and indicate that Dr. Dollar was quite receptive to student questions no matter what was going on.

3. Dr. Dollar often asked some very good Analysis level questions (4a) during his class; however, because he never left any "wait-time" (10 - Silence) after them, the students didn't have time to think of an answer and he wound up answering them himself. (There were three tallies in the 4-10 cell of the matrix for this class and twenty-six tallies in the 4-5 cell.)

4. This class session included a great deal of extended "empathy" (see the 1-1 cell on the matrix) and a lot of positive reinforcement (see the 8-2 cell) during the discussion of the problem solutions. This gave the students support and positive feelings about their accomplishments.

5. In addition, there were *no* 5m codes recorded during the entire class.

Conclusion

Throughout my consultation with Dr. Dollar he was always very open to my suggestions and incorporated most of them in his teaching. He carefully studied each set of data sheets and the matrix for each class session. He indicated that becoming aware of the types of interaction he was using in the class made him much more cognizant of the part the students need to play in the teaching-learning process.

Around mid-term I conducted a verbal evaluation in both of his classes and we found that his rapport with the students was now very good. Even though he still didn't hold office hours, as such, they felt he was accessible and concerned about their learning. In addition, the averages on his Course/Instructor Survey for the Fall semester went up quite dramatically — most were at .7 and above. Though not among the top ratings for most classes, we discovered that his averages for the "global items" were the *highest ever* for anyone who had taught *that* course. (The students *really* hated it!!)

In addition to the students' positive feelings about Dr. Dollar and the course, he discovered that he actually enjoyed teaching the course *and* found, by getting to know some of them, that his students were bright and stimulating! Dr. Dollar has since been promoted to full Professor, has subsequently taught "the" course to a mob of 440, and was awarded the Mass Section Teaching Award in the College of Business.

The Cognitive Interaction Analysis System (CIAS) has been used for eight years to help identify "communication problems" in university classrooms. It seems to help faculty members realize that they are teaching students and not just content. They also begin to think in terms of interaction patterns which can be used to communicate their objectives most effectively. As consultants we need to incorporate tools and techniques which will catch the interest of our clients as well as provide concrete evidence that something *has* been accomplished! The CIAS can do both of these things.

References

Flanders, N.A. (1970). *Analyzing teaching behavior*. Reading, Mass.: Addison-Wesley Publishing Company.

Johnson, G.R. (1978). *Johnson's cognitive interaction analysis system and computer program*. Unpublished manuscript. (Available from: Dr. Glenn R. Johnson, Center for Teaching Excellence, Texas A&M University, College Station, TX 77843-4246.)

For additional information about the Expanded CIAS or to obtain a copy of *Monitoring Your Classroom Communication Skills* (A Programed Workbook and Audiocassette for Developing Coding Skills using Johnson's Cognitive Interaction Analysis System (CIAS) and Expanded CIAS) please contact:

> Dr. Karron G. Lewis
> Center for Teaching Effectiveness
> Main Building 2200
> The University of Texas at Austin
> Austin, Texas 78712-1111
> Ph: (512) 471-1488

For information about the CIAS training module software (for IBM PC and compatible) contact:

> Dr. Glenn Ross Johnson
> Center for Teaching Excellence
> Texas A&M University
> College Station, Texas 77843-4246
> Ph: (409) 845-8392

Karron G. Lewis is a Faculty Development Specialist at the Center for Teaching Effectiveness, University of Texas at Austin. Her academic background is in Music Education and the Observation and Analysis of Classroom Interactions. She has been in faculty development realted activities since 1973. She developed the Expanded CIAS system which is described in this chapter and uses it extensively in individual consultation. She welcomes comments and may be reached at: The Center for Teaching Effectiveness, Main Building 2200, The University of Texas at Austin, Austin, TX 78712-1111. (512) 471-1488

Consultation with Video: Memory Management through Stimulated Recall

David Taylor-Way
Instructional Support Services
Cornell University

At a luncheon for new faculty we had set up, one of a series entitled "The Art of Teaching," a faculty member who was on the program turned to me while we were eating and asked, "So tell me, how did you get to be the guru of good teaching at Cornell?" After getting over my initial reaction to the question (*Guru? Me? I'm nobody's Guru.*) I had to disillusion him on the nature of my role as an instructional consultant. His quip masks an attitude that says, "Hey, who are you to tell me how to teach?" or to put it another way, "I don't know much about improving my teaching but I know when it works."

Of course it is not difficult to see where this attitude comes from, nor is it difficult to empathize with. Teaching to the teacher is like religion or sex: it is fundamentally a very personal matter. Considering that the average postsecondary faculty member has had very little, at best, formal help learning how to teach, how are we to address the problem that postsecondary teaching can and should be continually improved, revitalized and developed?

I have been concerned with this state of affairs for the last twelve years. During that time I have come to some conclusions, experimented with various techniques, collected data in different forms, and practiced and honed my consultation skills to the point that I believe I can put this accumulation of knowledge and experience to some coherent form.

Some Basic Assumptions

A central part of my method of consultation involves what I call *videotape-recall* (Taylor-Way, 1981). Videotape-recall uses videotape technology to record a sample of the teacher's classroom behavior. That record is then used by the consultant to stimulate the teacher to recall what he or she was thinking or feeling during significant classroom episodes. This method builds on early work with stimulated recall (Bloom, 1953) and counseling work with "Interpersonal Process Recall" (Kagan, 1975). In addition, it is driven by components of a theory of educating (Gowin, 1981), learning theory (Novak, 1977), and educational psychology (Ausubel, Novak & Hanesian, 1978). I feel strongly that if a consultant is going to take on the task of helping faculty improve their teaching skills, in whatever form (hopefully not as a guru) the consultant should have a theoretical framework to act as a guiding force. I'm not advocating working from one set theory, but borrowing from existing theories with the epistemological understanding that theories evolve, they are not written in stone and should change as our knowledge and experience grow. The best way to see how the theories I mentioned earlier fit together is through the following relational diagram:

[Consultant <--> {Teacher <--> (Students <--> Subject Matter)}]

(NOTE: I am indebted to Donald Schon for the above diagram.)

In the above diagram, we see the need for learning theory in the consultation process when the subject of the students' learning the material comes up while reviewing the videotape. Learning theory is also relevant for the teacher who is presumably learning how to modify teaching practice. Counseling theory has proven to me to be crucial in the outermost relationship above, that between the consultant and teacher. Theories of educational psychology and educating have been useful guides to my consultation when considering the entire set of relationships above: we are dealing with an educative experience for the teacher, for the teacher's students and for the consultant, who is also learning about consulting.

Several assumptions underlie the videotape recall method:

- first, that the act of improving, analyzing, reflecting on and evaluating one's teaching should be *event*--oriented (we are dealing with what teachers *do*, not just with what they *say* they do);

- second, we need a reliable and detailed record to work from;

- third, everything a teacher says or does, both in preparation for teaching, and in class, is functionally related to how they think about teaching, what they are thinking at any moment in the classroom, and how they are feeling.

- Finally, there is the fact, based on research evidence (Shavelson & Stern, 1981; Clark & Yinger, 1977), that teachers learn how to deal with the myriad complexities of the act of teaching by a system of short-term memory management.

I will discuss these assumptions in more detail later in this chapter. Working from these assumptions, having a theoretical basis, and using videotape all have come to be indispensable components of the relative effectiveness of my consulting work with postsecondary faculty.

Let me go back to the attitude problem I mentioned in the first paragraph. New and experienced faculty have a different set of problems they face in the act of learning about their teaching. Any effort aimed at influencing that process must take into account the individual teacher's experience, personality, style, needs and motivation. I agree with others (Nyquist, 1986) that the "ownership" of the consultation process must be with the teacher in question. Therefore to use videotape requires, from the start, the cooperation and willingness of that teacher. For those too threatened by being videotaped I use other approaches in the consultation process, such as classroom visitation without video, or just meeting with the faculty member in my office to discuss what he or she wishes. The majority of the faculty I work with, however, are willing to be videotaped right from the beginning. In other cases, we may not start out with the idea of using videotape, but once we have framed a set of goals or problems, it frequently becomes clear that videotaping would give us a much better handle on things.

The Recording Process

Once the decision has been made to go ahead with the videotaping I will schedule a day to tape the teacher, so he or she knows in advance. In spite of the possibility that advance knowledge of the taping date may influence performance, I believe that the advantages of a cooperative and up-front approach more than compensate for it. I have been experimenting with videotape technology since 1971 and have continually upgraded the hardware I use as the industry has continued to improve image quality, audio options, and most importantly, equipment size and portability. My most recent upgrade has resulted in my using a very small camcorder, slightly larger than a typical 35mm camera, that focuses itself, has power-zoom and battery power. I set up within two or three minutes in the back of the classroom, behind the students, or to one side. This is the only consideration I make to being inconspicuous. I feel this approach is far more ethically justifiable than hiding behind something like a two-way mirror. It also means I am recording in a "natural" situation and am not inconveniencing anyone by requiring them to move their class somewhere special to accommodate recording hardware limitations.

I then proceed to record the first twenty minutes of the class. I limit the recording to twenty minutes because the videotape recall process can be a very "dense" experience: you can get a lot out of very little. We rarely get through twenty minutes of tape in the hour I limit the review session to. I limit the review to an hour because I don't want to incur any more of a cost of the teacher's time than that. We can still accomplish a great deal in an hour. In addition, I don't want to overburden the teacher with too many new ideas all at once.

While recording I make sure I focus on what the teacher is doing at all times. I usually keep zoomed into wide-angle during interactive sequences so we can see who is saying what, and zoomed into telephoto if the blackboard, overhead or other visuals are being used. My position in the room, the compactness of my equipment and the fact that the teacher has invited my attendance, all combine to minimize the influence of my presence on the classroom environment. The camcorder technology of today allows recording in light situations of down to 7 lux (equivalent to the light from a cigarette lighter at approximately a yard away). What this means is that the teacher may use overheads, slides or any other a/v equipment that requires darkening the room. A decent level of contrast may still be maintained on the video recording without the need for special lighting.

The audio quality is at least, if not more important, as the quality of the visual recording. I do not place a lot of microphones around the room, nor have I had to use a wireless microphone. One super-directional microphone attached to the camcorder, or placed within my reach, is sufficient. In huge lecture halls where I may have to sit farther from the teacher than usual, there will be a PA system used in most cases which is enough to amplify the teacher for adequate recording quality. The major drawback is that under these conditions, student questions or responses will not pick up unless they are within a fifteen foot radius of the super-directional mike.

After the twenty minute tape runs out, I pack up my equipment and begin taking general, descriptive notes for the rest of the class. Note-taking involves writing down verbatim specific interactions I feel are significant to focus on during the consultation process, or general characteristics about pacing, use of silence, level of abstraction and other pertinent teaching concepts. At the end of the class I will schedule a review session with the teacher, if I haven't already done so, hopefully within 24 hours of the recording.

Reviewing the Recording

The teacher and I meet in my office to review the video recording within 24 hours, while the teacher's memory of the class is reasonably fresh. We use the videotape recording to reconstruct covert events: what and how the teacher was thinking and feeling during the class. I am concerned with teacher's thoughts and feelings for several reasons. First, they provide a focal point. Other experiments using videotape to review a person's behavior suggest there is a "cosmetic effect" (Allen & Ryan, 1969; Carrol, 1976) which must be overcome when that person first sees their tape. A person reviewing their behavior on video has to learn how to relate to their videotaped image. This learning is necessary because of previous experience watching television, which is a very passive experience. Watching oneself on video in the context of videotape recall requires the teacher to take a very active role, otherwise it is easy to become mesmerized.

Another thing the teacher is learning during the early videotape reviews is what to look for, what aspects of his or her teaching are significant and what behaviors are insignificant for the improvement of practice. The first part of the consultant's job in videotape recall involves helping the teacher focus on the significant aspects of his or her teaching. Using the videotape as a recall stimulus to allow the teacher to make connections between how he or she was thinking, feeling and acting helps to highlight the more significant teaching sequences.

Focusing on the covert processes also avoids a shallow behavioral approach to the improvement of teaching. Research on teacher thinking (MacKay & Marland, 1978) suggests a direct connection between how teachers *think* about teaching, including how they plan and make decisions "in flight" (Joyce, B., 1978-79) and what they *do* in the act of teaching. Ultimately, the teacher will be making decisions to change certain actions, either what they do in preparation for teaching, or how they handle certain regularities in class. Those actions are functionally related to the teacher's thinking and feelings, so by helping the teacher to make specific connections between thinking, feeling and acting, the consultant is working on a much more fundamental level than simply changing behaviors.

The consultant working to help a teacher improve his or her instruction must keep in mind the relationship between the teacher's affective, cognitive and behavioral learning. We talk about them separately only for convenience. Referring to the physiological makeup of the brain, Kagan says "Cognition is bathed in a sea of affective fluids." (Kagan, 1987), or, to use Shulman's phrasing, "Cognition is a matzo ball sitting in a chicken soup of affect." (Shulman, 1987). However you wish to think of this relationship, it is misleading for the consultant to discuss or even think of the teacher's thoughts, feelings or actions as if they were totally discrete phenomena. The consultant focusing only on changing behaviors runs the risk of limiting the teacher's learning to merely knowing what to do, but not knowing why it should be done, or when (lacking the wisdom necessary to judge appropriateness of action). On the other hand, focusing only on changing the way the teacher thinks or feels about a certain teaching act, or while carrying it out, runs the risk of limiting the teacher's learning to knowing what to do, when and why to do it, but lacking the ability to carry it out behaviorally (lacking the artistic quality of skillful practice). The complexity of these relationships has profound implications for assessing both the teacher's progress in the improvement of teaching and the consultant's skill in empowering that improvement.

Videotape recall begins with the consultant spending a few minutes explaining the recall process with the teacher before playing back the tape. It might begin with an introduction like:

> In order to help you get the most out of this experience we have to know what to focus on. One way to help you get a handle on why you do certain things under specific conditions is to see how your thinking and feelings affect your actions. What I'd like you to do is try to recall as much as you can about what you were thinking, either about the subject matter - what you were trying to get across, the thoughts behind the words - or the process, what your intentions or objectives were, what you expected from the students. I'm also interested in your feelings: were you enthusiastic, frustrated, anxious, having fun, feelings like that. As you watch, try to bring these things to mind and then tell me to stop the tape whenever you

recall anything. Don't worry about whether it may be important or not, just stop as often as you can.

This short introduction is usually enough to get things started. If the teacher hasn't stopped the tape within five minutes or so, I will put it on pause and ask something like, "Anything happening yet?" or "How's it going so far?" I'm very conscious of getting the *teacher* to stop the tape, rather than continually stopping it myself, so I know we are talking about things he or she is interested in. This is one way of keeping the "ownership" of the session with the teacher and avoids creating a dependency where the teacher learns to rely on me to choose when to stop the tape. Once I get the teacher talking about things and reflecting, my role changes from getting the teacher to stop the tape to my asking open-ended, probing questions (see "Consultant's leads for use in Videotape Recall" at the end of this chapter to get an idea of the kind of questions I ask the teacher). My questioning is aimed at helping the teacher to conceptualize his or her teaching. This is where having the detailed video record is crucial and where the reconstruction of the covert record of thoughts and feelings helps bring out regularities. If the teacher can begin to recognize patterns in their teaching (leaving insufficient wait time, ineffective warm-up, answering their own questions, pacing too fast or slow), they can begin to name those patterns in order to refine the way they think about those teaching actions. This is what I mean by "conceptualizing" the teaching process.

Once teachers can begin to put into words what they are doing, their thinking about the process of teaching becomes more abstract, which can have disadvantages in that subtle nuances of context can be lost. It is also, however, a more efficient way of thinking, which is, in my experience, an advantage. The potential disadvantage of the abstractness can be compensated for by the consultant through the construction of principles of teaching. I use the expression "principle of teaching," meaning a very personal construct that is a "guide to action" (Gowin, 1981, 128).

Other researchers working in different paradigms have used different words such as "moves" (Bellack, et.al., 1966), or "scripts" (Shank & Abelson, 1977). The use of these various terms reflects the different research paradigm of the authors. Bellack and his associates conceptualized the various interactive patterns of classroom teaching as a "game" in which teacher and students made different "moves." Schank & Abelson were more concerned with the cognitive antecedents to overt teaching behaviors and conceptualized the teacher's decision-making process as a system for effectively accessing into short term memory various "scripts," which were learned behavioral patterns residing in long-term memory. It is the idea that the process of learning how to teach and improve one's teaching begins with a cognitive process dealing with memory management that I think is important to the consultation process using videotape recall.

I'm less interested in whether the consultant's framework is based on moves, scripts, or strategies than I am that the consultation process address the relationship between how a teacher thinks, feels and acts in regards to teaching. To do that the consultant must deal with the teacher's learning memory, which I think is best handled through a three-step process:

1. *focusing* on a specific, discrete pattern or regularity, presumably where there is a discrepancy between what the teacher sees on the videotape, and what the teacher thinks is a more preferable approach,

2. giving a name *(conceptualizing)* that pattern or regularity,

3. *reframing* or developing with the guidance of the consultant, a strategy or principle of how to reduce the discrepancy between thought (or feeling) and action.

I will go into the theoretical basis for this process in more detail shortly. I prefer to use the term principle of teaching, rather than strategy. Shulman's work (Shulman, 1986) makes a more careful distinction between these two terms than I am able to in this chapter.

Whereas a strategy of teaching is more generic, such as "warm up," "wait time," or "summarizing," a principle of teaching is an individualized way of dealing with that generic regularity. An example of a *principle* for warming up in a foreign language class might be that you would plan to engage students in casual conversation in the language being taught as they enter the classroom. An example of a *principle* you might use to ensure enough wait time after asking a question for students to respond effectively is to count silently to yourself from one to five, or seven. An example of a *principle* to deal with effective summarizing might be to budget time into your lesson plan at the end of the period and to review briefly the major concepts that have been covered, but in a fresh way. Of course there are many other principles to deal with each of these situations and it is the objective of the consultant to encourage the teacher to come up with various principles to be prepared and more flexible in responding to the complexities and variables of the teaching situation.

Theoretical Basis

The theoretical basis for generating principles (or strategies) is to help free up the working, short-term memory of the teacher so he or she has more available memory to monitor the teaching process. Gaea Leinhardt's work (Leinhardt, 1983) comparing novice and experienced, effective teachers suggests that one primary distinguishing characteristic of the expert is that he or she has not only one, but a variety of schemas (her term for what I've been calling principles) to use as teaching tools for a specific kind of teaching episode. This concept is important because it suggests that as consultants we can assist not only novices by helping them write out some of their first teaching principles, but also the experienced teacher who may be faced with a situation where all the standard principles they have come to rely upon do not work.

If the teacher's working memory is a chaotic jumble of information consisting of internally and externally supplied cues with no apparent pattern, no filter to reveal the underlying regularity, how can the teacher effectively respond to a complex and unanticipated classroom situation? The problem may be one of propriety: the teacher is using a well-conceived principle inappropriately, like getting students to respond to each other in a discussion, rather than just to the teacher, but failing to focus or summarize what is being said. If the teacher is continually stumbling to come up with effective responses to each new teaching situation, it may be he or she is not capable of fulfilling the more global, but essential function of monitoring the classroom process to see if their objectives are being met.

The idea of monitoring the process applies even to a strict lecture situation. How often have we been witness to the lecturer who rushes through the material seemingly oblivious to the students: whether they look bored, confused, whether they have time to take adequate notes. In this case the teacher's working memory has been filled with the subject matter, probably on purpose, because to accommodate all the cues available from the students would be an overload for the teacher's short term memory. Such a teacher has no principles by which to get across the information while simultaneously monitoring the process.

By starting and stopping the videotape, the consultant's objective is to get the teacher, first to recall what thoughts and/or feelings may be governing their classroom actions, and second, to put into words any previously unarticulated teaching principles. The next step is to help the teacher devise new and additional principles which may be more effective for a given situation, and add them to his or her repertoire. I generally reserve the last five to ten minutes of the consultation hour to review our discussion of the videotape. Depending on the teacher's experience and my sense of how open he or she is to experimentation, I may give him or her a form to fill out and return to me as soon as possible. This form is a formal way to get them to reflect on the recall experience and to begin to formulate the principles of teaching that came out of it. (See **Figure 1**.)

In spite of the fact that the use of such a form may seem somewhat mechanical, it can serve a very critical function in the consultation process. It is the primary way I have of assessing the effectiveness of the consultation. It tells me

VIDEOTAPE RECALL FORM

Instructions: Please take time to fill this form out carefully after your videotape recall session. Your objective is to formulate the significant points that came out of discussing your teaching into clearly phrased principles of teaching which you can use during your subsequent teaching to refine it. A principle is a "guide to action" and as such should be in the form of a statement dealing with what you must do, rather than being limited to what you want to change. An example would be, "I realize I must pace things faster, so I will write reminders in my notes to keep the pace up. I will also pay particular attention to my interactive rhythm with my students." After you fill out this form, make a copy and put it in my mailbox, [keep the original for future reference].

Instructor: **Date:**

What concept (regularity in events) of teaching am I dealing with?

_____

_____

_____

_____

What cues, either internal (that I supply to myself), or external (supplied by the students or situation) define the conditions and context of the concepts?

_____

_____

_____

_____

What principle(s) can guide me in effectively dealing with the situation?

_____

_____

_____

_____

Figure 1. Videotape Recall Form

whether the teacher has been able to devise a set of principles from the experience and it is a reference by which I can then verify, through subsequent classroom visits and recall sessions, the degree of success of the teacher's improvement in performance. Sometimes a bit of fine-tuning is required, which can be done through further consultation, with or without the need for videotaping.

Filling out the form facilitates the active learning process for the teacher — conceptualizing the teaching episode and devising a set of principles is a start. Even if no fine-tuning is required, practice and experimentation will be necessary before the teacher has truly learned how to solve the problem. However, the teacher has made a very substantial start which has been of his or her own creation and which has accommodated the underlying cognitive and affective processes involved. Let me illustrate through a case study transcription.

Case Study Illustration

What follows is a transcript of a videotape recall session with a first year graduate teaching assistant in philosophy. He had very little teaching experience but was very motivated to not only teach well, but to benefit from the consultation process. I had already met with him several times before the particular session transcribed below. The first time we met he practiced teaching in a microteaching session which was videotaped. The purpose of the microteaching was to teach him the videotape recall process. Such a microteaching session may not be absolutely necessary with all faculty clients, but I usually include one with the TAs I work with to help "demystify" the videotaping process.

The second time I met with this particular TA was a little over a month before the session transcribed below. That was his first videotape recall session and we begin the session that follows by discussing what he got out of it. Key statements by the teacher which I use to focus the consultation process are in italics.

Consultant: To start things off, maybe you can just talk a little about what kind of progress you've made on these things and maybe where you need to go. The first one in terms of preparation (reading from recall form): "[I] Should concentrate not on collecting enough material to fill the hour (never yet a problem!) — but on planning a clear, but flexible structure, including (1) introduction of material — main issues and how related, (2) key question(s), (3) main point(s) for summary.

Teacher: Generally, I certainly have changed the way I prepare because, to start with, to a greater extent than I do now, I was just trying to think of all the things I could bring in that would be relevant, if I needed to, because I may have finished saying what I wanted to say about something else, or there wasn't any discussion going and I'd run out of things to say. And I've stopped doing that to a large extent and tended much more to concentrate on having relatively few. In fact, the notes I have prepared have tended to get smaller, but they're a coherent set, refined to one sentence each. Then I'll have some key issue related to that, which is an attempt to get them wanting to start asking me questions, or talk about something that's a problem, something that I face them with, rather than explaining. I tend to do that, and then have some way of continuing to talk about that if they're still obviously confused and just need more explanation in such a way that although I can continue talking about it but they're not willing to participate. What I'm now saying is continuing to give them a chance to participate by presenting them questions or problems.

The other thing is I do try to indicate on my notes in capital letters, telling myself to stop early enough to summarize. *That sort of planning, how well it works, depends on how they respond because the sections where I've had the best discussion are where I've deliberately attempted to make them get into a discussion between themselves and succeeded in doing that.* So it's tended to be that I've hardly even finished my little bit of introductory stuff about what we ought to be discussing in this class when they're already sticking up their hands and saying, "But what about this..." and the thing gets going of its own accord without my even trying. It runs on, runs on and goes fine and then we're running out of time and just at the end I'll say, "We're running out of time, but look how we've covered this, this, this, and it's very easy to do that. *Yesterday, and in some of the other sections, particularly earlier in the semester, were examples where it didn't work because when I got to the end of what I'd prepared for introductory material I could already tell that they weren't very happy with the material, or they hadn't done the readings, or something like that and that I needed to say more, so I continued on a bit asking them questions, but I wasn't getting much response and so I was then slightly unsure of what to do, or at least I continued on in that way, so that was less effective.*

Consultant: But you're more conscious of summarizing, more conscious of closure at the end.

Teacher: Yeah.

Consultant: Good! [Reading] "Using key questions and questions about students' responses to build momentum, then allow any student-to-student interaction to flourish <u>before</u> intervening again."

Teacher: That's something we picked up from the last tape, that *I'd been so concerned about getting the discussion going that I killed the discussion.* I have been really conscious of that and have tried hard to *resist the temptation, which is still there,* to elaborate on what a student says, give them the "right" answer before somebody else talks, so I try to stop myself doing that.

Consultant: Have you been getting more student-to-student interaction?

Teacher: Yeah.

Consultant: So you feel like you've been making progress?

Teacher: Yeah.

Consultant: OK. Then the last thing here, [reading] "Longer pauses! Must not give the students the impression that I think my questions to them are merely rhetorical. Encourage them to take questions literally and answer."

Teacher: That's something that I certainly noticed yesterday that I wasn't doing. *Something I need to work out is the temptation to worry about pauses — that's very strong. I think that's something I still haven't overcome. I've got to work on that. I noticed several times yesterday, and we'll see on the tape, that I got to the end of the question and instead of just stopping and waiting for an answer, as soon as I worried after 10 seconds and nobody was immediately coming in with a response, I started re-explaining the question, putting it another way, not moving on because I wanted them to have a chance to think about it, trying to mark time while they thought about it, but continuing to speak while I'm marking time, and I wasn't really intending to do that.*

Consultant: Well, that's one of the things that can come out of today, is fine-tuning some of these things. We've obviously got some areas you've been focusing on and we can do several things: we can see, literally on the tape, where you see progress having been made — you can point that out to me. But also you might discover where you might need to fine tune. On the form you fill out for today you might need to fill out some more specific notes to yourself about fine tuning...

In the case of this particular teacher we can see he has come to the second recall session having had very specific focal points. If this were his first recall session we would have begun by my explaining the nature of the recall process and instructed him to stop the tape, based on covert information he was able to recall (see page 165 above).

The teacher's comments indicate he has been conscious of having made changes and noted progress on specific problems. He has also indicated that there are other contingencies where he is still unsure of what to do. In these cases he may very well need to either "fine tune" the principles he has already developed, or create some additional ones.

It's important to realize that all of these outcomes of the teacher's experience with the consultation process have happened as a result of a very brief relationship with the consultant, in this case only three sessions of an hour each, one of which was based on a very artificial microteaching situation. One of my consulting objectives is to provide the teacher with as focused and powerful an experience in as short a time as possible. My role is to help the teacher focus on a discrete and manageable set of issues, conceptualize those issues and reframe them by creating principles of teaching to empower the teacher in dealing with them more effectively. Clearly then, the teacher has the large responsibility of creating his or her own principles. This is a consultation paradigm which is "inquiry-oriented," one which "recognizes the individual's ability to analyze his or her own teaching" (Zeichner, 1983).

If the teacher is relatively inexperienced, as in this case, the process of conceptualizing and reframing more than likely will require continual refinement. The early phases of the process involve becoming more aware of the pattern of behavior and its relationship with covert processes. It is important for the consultant to reinforce any progress, however minute, that the teacher feels in order to avoid discouragement, maintain motivation and also to be realistic in not representing the process of instructional improvement as "quick fix." Many teachers may expect a "quick fix" or "miraculous cure" from the consultant as a doctor or guru and it should be emphasized that teachers can "cure" themselves.

A reassuring thing in the above transcription is that the teacher is able to articulate the problem: "I noticed several times yesterday, and we'll see on the tape, that I got to the end of the question and instead of just stopping and waiting for an answer..." I am quick to pick up on this in my last comment, point it out to the teacher and encourage him by stating what we can do about it during the second recall session.

Teacher: (stopping tape) *This is going on much longer than I remembered it. While you're talking or explaining something, time passes much quicker than you think it does.* I really intended to be talking like this for about 5 minutes and it went on longer than that.

Consultant: Are you saying that you're doing more talking than you'd like to?

Teacher: I think that it looks to me like what I should concentrate on here is keeping the introduction more condensed and shorter and turning some of this material that I'm just explaining into questions, trying to use it more to start the discussion, ask them more questions.

Consultant: Why do you think you did it the way you did?

Teacher: *Um (pause) probably because* I think that, at least for me, *I find it easier just to lecture,* because I understand the material very well and I don't have any problem talking in a reasonably coherent way about it. I could very easily go in there and just talk for 50 minutes and give them a lecture, but that's not what I want to do. But in a way *that's easier than getting discussion going and thinking about how best to provoke discussion —* make them learn from their own interactions with each other.

Consultant: Are you saying it's easier to lecture because you don't have to coax something out of somebody else?

Teacher: Yeah, I think so.

Consultant: Do you recall how you were feeling at this point, or how you feel in general under these conditions? I guess what I'm trying to get at is, do you feel good, or better, when you're lecturing?

Teacher: *I don't feel better when I'm lecturing than when there's a good discussion going.* I don't mind at all just sitting back and letting them talk with a little controlling focus on my part. *I definitely feel better lecturing than I do at that point where I'm sort of trying to coax discussion out of them when not much is happening.* So it's easier to just explain stuff and I think *I succumb to that temptation subconsciously,* just by going on really longer than I ought to.

Consultant: You just said something very important when you used the word "subconsciously," which tells me that you're not that aware of this. That's why I asked you about your feeling because looking at you — I don't know if you're picking this up from the tape — but looking at you, both on the tape and when I was actually there, I get a definite sense of energy from you and I'm wondering if that's part of what's going on is you're really cranking on and there's this energy behind your words, and that influences the way you're interacting or not.

Teacher: Yeah.

Consultant: If *that's* the case, if part of it has to do with a feeling of energy, then I suspect in order to do something about the quality of interaction, you need to deal with this feeling.

Teacher: Right.

Consultant: That's something you may need to think about, unless you have some ideas now about it.

Teacher: I can certainly channel it into just directing the discussion between the students when that happens. I think that the energy comes from the thought that it's exciting material and it's interesting to try and explain it. *It's genuinely exciting when you succeed in explaining it and it's clear that things are getting across, and so on. That can come either from lecturing or from having them discuss stuff and realizing in a subtle way you are succeeding in controlling the way the discussion's going. They're really doing the work and you're just sort of holding the rudder.* I find that exciting and easy to do, whereas *I immediately start feeling much more unsure of myself when I'm trying to get them to start doing it and nothing's happening.*

Consultant: OK. Now you said that when you're trying to get them started, are you implying that once they've started, it's easier at that point?

Teacher: Yeah.

Consultant: OK. So it looks like what we're talking about is getting it started.

Teacher: Um hum.

Consultant: What is so difficult for you about getting it started?

Teacher: Um, I think it's that sometimes it starts very much of its own while I'm still finishing explaining something and they just start asking questions or disagreeing with what I'm saying and things just get going and I don't have to think about it.

Consultant: So *then* it's not a problem.

Teacher: Right.

Consultant: So then when *is* it a problem?

Teacher: When it is a problem *I suppose I just feel...um...in some way that I find it hard to define. I feel much more uncertain about my ability to, in a constructive way, get sort of a transition from my talking to their talking* which is definitely a transition I want to take place. If the initial response I get from asking what seem to me to be pertinent and interesting questions that ought to elicit a response, then *I start to worry I'm going to lose the group.*

Consultant: OK, it sounds to me like you are missing some information that helps you distinguish the difference between when it works and gets going on its own and when it doesn't.

Teacher: Um hum.

Consultant: I also suspect that what we need to do is to look carefully at the tape and see if you can pick out some places where maybe you have seen it appropriate to get some discussion going, but where it wasn't and then stop it and tell me what you could have done at that point that you weren't doing.

Teacher: OK.

Consultant: (starts tape)

Here we're getting much more focused. The teacher begins by recognizing the fundamental fact of time distortion in teaching. I try to reinforce his perception by paraphrasing it, "... you're doing more talking than you'd like to?" I then focus on the potential underlying causes, "Why do you think you did it the way you did?" The fact that he pauses before replying and begins with an "Umm" indicates that he may not yet see any connection between his behavior and covert processes. The fact that he qualifies his response with a "probably" is an indicator for the consultant to recognize that he may not be truly *recalling* the underlying cause of his behavior but *attributing* a plausible cause to it. I try to steer him away from that line of thinking by the use of another paraphrase, "Are you saying it's easier to lecture because you don't have to coax something out of somebody...?" I then explore the possibility that there is an underlying feeling he may be governed by. He points out he feels better when there is a discussion going than when he is lecturing (something I want to reinforce), but that he feels better lecturing than trying to coax the students to talk. We are getting much more focused now. I'm hoping he is beginning to see how his feelings are governing his behavior and I point out that up until now he has not been aware of his feelings. His speech is rapid and intense on the tape and I give him my own interpretation of this ("... I get a definite sense of energy from you...") to explore whether we can "name" a feeling (conceptualize it).

My next move as a consultant is to help him come to terms with the feeling. I am also careful to provide positive reinforcement whenever dealing with a teacher's feelings "...there's nothing wrong with that. We know your students rated you high on enthusiasm..." This points out the value of student mid-term evaluation data on teaching during the consultation process. I have the teacher administer a questionnaire half-way through the semester, between the two recall sessions, to act as a sort of validating factor. It allows me to point out where the observations and conclusions the teacher and I draw in the consultation process can be validated by the students' own opinions.

I then throw the ball back to the teacher and give him first option at developing a principle of teaching to help him deal with his feelings. If I made a suggestion here or gave him some advice, my feeling is he may or may not follow it since he did not generate it. I also avoid giving advice right away to avoid creating a dependency relationship between the consultant and the teacher.

We get even more focused when we get to the point of his exploring why the initiating part of leading the discussion is difficult. He is able to tell me the conditions when he has no problem but seems a bit more hesitant describing the exact conditions of the problem. His association of feeling uncertain under certain, as yet undefined, conditions will be a focal point later on in the consultation process. I then focus the teacher very specifically before we turn the tape back on. I'm hoping the teacher can pick out a specific instance of the situation which will tell me he is beginning to define it, and then challenge him, in the luxury and safety of the private recall session, to develop an alternate response to the situation.

Teacher: Right here is exactly what I was saying before, *I should have just stopped and asked a question, but I kept on adding bits and qualifying and changing it because I could already see they were still at a relatively unresponsive stage because there were no hands shooting up or people looking like they wanted to speak. So I knew that if I just stopped there would have been silence.*

Consultant: OK, I suspect that there's two things going on here. It is safe to say that you're still establishing the context of discussion, or have you already done that?

Teacher: I think I've already done that. This is a question I'm formulating here which is saying, "Here is, in a nutshell, what the problem is. What do you think?"

Consultant: Had you planned that?

Teacher: Yes.

Consultant: Had you planned that specifically? I mean, in other words, had you planned things so specifically that you had the exact thing written down as to how you were going to initiate discussion?

Teacher: *Um, more or less.* I had formulated in my mind what the dilemma was.

Consultant: That's an issue thing, I'm thinking about a mechanism thing, either in the form of a specific question, or...

Teacher: Um, I think I'd got it this specific that I was just going to say, "Right. Here's the question. Here's what the dilemma is. Somebody tell me what they think, tell me what they would do in this situation?" But *it may be that I hadn't got it specific enough in the sense that I had a question written down. That would have stopped me...*

Consultant: You see I'm thinking that if there's a mechanism that you can create for yourself to get that initiated, because that seems to be what you're struggling with is the initiation part of it, not once it gets going. It seems to me that in the absence of having a specific thing, either question, or task that you can give them, you have a tendency to keep talking.

Teacher: Yeah.

Consultant: So what I'm suggesting is one possible solution would be in the planning, which was the first item from your first session, that you include the mechanism, explicitly planned.

Teacher: Yeah.

Consultant: Do you suppose that if you had a good question there and you had asked it, right at this point here (indicated tape), and then just shut up, what do you think would have happened?

Teacher: *Um, I think if I had shut up long enough I would have got a response, eventually.*

Consultant: Would there have been a problem in doing that?

Teacher: Um, no, *it's just that I would be strongly tempted, that stopping and waiting is a difficult thing to do, I feel awkward.*

Consultant: Whenever you change modes of instruction, from presentation to discussion, you're dealing with inertia. I think we talked about this last time. Part of why you might think they're getting sleepy while you're initiating the discussion is because they have been in a passive mode. They're not just going to overcome that passive inertia right away. So it's reasonable to assume that that may require some waiting on your part. This is not an unusual problem for people and what I've suggested to some people is, if the waiting feels awkward, one thing you can do is to give yourself something to do while you are pausing.

I think it's important to maintain eye contact during that time so you can recognize people. But there are several other things you can do. One thing is just scan: look at faces. Do they look confused, or alert? Or you might be thinking of a follow-up question, a probe, because it's possible that your first question might not hit the mark for them. It might be either too vague, or not focused enough, or they just might not be able to answer it. Clearly, part of the skill has to do with how good that first question is. So it's nice to be able to have the time to carefully plan that question ahead of time. The point is, give yourself something to do so your attention is less on yourself than it is on them and the material. I think the awkwardness comes from being aware of yourself. From the students' point of view, they're thinking about a response to your question, they're not thinking about you...

At the outset of this sequence I could see the teacher was indeed able to think of an alternate response to the situation, "I should have just stopped and asked a question..." and he has begun to specify the conditions of the situation which made him feel unsure of himself, "...there were no hands shooting up or people looking like they wanted to speak." My questions about his planning are an attempt to deal with his feeling unsure and awkward. I'm hoping to help him develop a technique that he can come to class prepared with, rather than just relying on the spur of the moment. His concentration on the dilemma indicates he may have no mechanism for dealing with the process of initiating the discussion from that dilemma. I try to point out he may need a mechanism, a specific question that he had prepared ahead of time to focus the students. This approach may help his confidence if he has a set of questions prepared ahead of time that he knows he wants answered.

I try to provide a conceptual framework to think about the problem of initiating discussion using the concepts of inertia and momentum. I also try to provide him with an action to take his attention off his feelings while he is waiting for the students to respond to his question. The fact that students are probably not thinking about _him_ as he's waiting for a response is something many people forget and may need to be reminded of.

We still have yet to get to the bottom of his feelings, however. We know developmentally his feelings may have to do with the locus of his concerns (Fuller, 1969). My feeling is it may help speed up the shift of concerns from the self to the students by focusing the teachers' attention away from themselves. This focusing can be done by helping identify specific cues they should be looking for. Being more focused on the students also involves recognizing they can contribute to the interactive process as well.

Consultant: What do you see going on here?

Teacher: (Laughs) *I see I'm still doing too much talking.* During this entire section I guess I could have done all of that by trying to coax those explanations out of them because it wasn't material they were completely unfamiliar with. But I didn't do that. I just carried on and explained them.

Consultant: There's another thing I'm wondering if you notice.

Teacher: Hmmm.

Consultant: You got two student questions here! Right?

Teacher: Yeah.

Consultant: So what does that tell you?

Teacher: *They're starting to get interested and they want to take off.*

Consultant: Right. Now, did you notice that then?

Teacher: *Umm, yeah, I did.* I actually broke off in mid-sentence because I saw that he raised his hand. *It's a funny conflict because on the one hand I was just talking when what I should have been doing was getting more discussion going. But on the other hand, as soon as I saw any opportunity arising, I sort of grabbed it. So I suppose that's partly explained by worrying about myself being able to get things going.*

Consultant: I think you just put your finger on it. You're worried that all this is on *you.*

Teacher: Umm, yeah.

Consultant: The burden is all on you and it really isn't. They're there as well and they can contribute. So maybe part of it has to do with you learning how to let go of that concern and see what happens. We know that if you remain silent for long enough, somebody will say something. If we know that will happen, and we've seen you do a good job of establishing the context here — you've got some things on the board — so they have a visual referent to go back to if they need, you've done your job! You probably know this from your own experience that once that momentum happens, once they pick the ball up and go with it, that puts you in a very different relationship with the class. Suddenly your role has changed dramatically from that point. You can't hang on to that lecture role, you have to switch roles. Possibly you've got two things going on. You've got this big concern about everything being on your shoulders in terms of your initiating it, but once it gets going you've got this need to fill in verbally.

Teacher: Yeah.

Consultant: If you could figure out a way of dealing with that it would not only help allowing them to give more input, but it might also affect who's talking. I'm wondering if you have any idea about that?

Teacher: *Umm...(pause)...yeah, well, I don't really have any clear idea of any specific means,* but just concentrate myself and realize *I not only can afford to but need* to talk less in certain situations in the classroom, and that *I can afford to and need* to not worry so much about things continuing on and just let them take the responsibility to a certain extent and let them generate some momentum.

Consultant: I think what you're going through is a very normal process that beginning teachers go through. Researchers who have studied teachers with varying levels of experience have found there is a gradual shift in concerns from the self for novice teachers, to the students, for experienced teachers. I'm wondering if there's something you can do to somehow relieve yourself of this burden? I'm hoping that over the semester you've gained some confidence.

Teacher: Yeah. *I can't think of anything specific* except to be very aware of it and keep it in mind.

Consultant: [Summarizing recall session discussion, seeking closure] I think we've talked about some very specific things that you can do. One thing that's very tangible is preparing questions ahead of time. If you came in with a set of prepared questions, it might make you feel a little more confident, then, be consistent about waiting, and see what happens. Also, remember that after you get the first response from a student, you don't have to react back immediately. There's an option there for a second wait time to see if some other student might want to react to that first response. That would help you deal with the initiating part of it. Then you'd also have this set of questions as a back-up, if nothing else. Does that sound like something that might help?

Teacher: Yeah. In fact on the first sheet there I wrote I should think up specific questions and write them down and *I think that's something I need to concentrate on even more than I realize.*

Consultant: Then another thing that we've talked about is when you are pausing, to focus outward, rather than inward. You might want to experiment with that to see whether that has any affect on you or not, whether that makes you feel any better;

experiment. Then the other thing we talked about is this sense
of energy that you have, which I think is a very positive thing
and your students are apparently picking up on it. It could
very well be that if we asked your students they wouldn't have
any major complaints about what's going on, so what we're
talking about here is talking about what you're doing in
relationship to what you want to be doing [fine tuning].

In the above sequence I begin by testing the teacher's
observation skills. Can he see what the problem is? Can he
think of an alternate response that might have been more
appropriate or effective? He is still thinking in terms of
himself, however, and in terms of coaxing, which possibly is
viewing the situation as more difficult than it really is. I'm
trying to get him to let go of his concern that the burden of
discussion lies solely with the teacher. He is beginning to
recognize that the chances are, if he waits long enough,
somebody else will say something.

It also may be the case he has no conception of more
than one role as a discussion leader. He is unaware of the need
for the teacher to play a more verbally passive, monitoring
role once the momentum has increased. Having framed the
problem now, I check to see where his thinking is in terms of
a solution. He clearly needs to reflect more on the situation, "I
don't really have any clear idea of any specific means...."

I then try to help his confidence by putting his problem
in a larger perspective, helping him realize that he is not the
only one who has faced this problem. Indeed, I'm sure this is
one of the most commonly occurring problems that new
teachers face, how to generate a true discussion and many
reading this will sympathize with this case.

This particular teacher seems to have a hard time
recognizing the principles of teaching we had discussed during
the consultation process. I always reserve the last five minutes
or so at the end of the session to review what we have
accomplished. In this case he had already indicated the need to
prepare key questions ahead of time from his first recall
session, but we see he had underestimated the need for
specificity in preparing those questions, evidence there is need
for his fine-tuning of that principle.

As a result of this session the teacher wrote the following principles to help guide the further refinement of dealing with the problems discussed during the consultation process:

1) <u>Problem:</u>   Introduction tends to run on into 20 minute lecture.

   <u>Solution:</u>   Define what must be introduced in lecture/explanation, from what can be introduced by asking students for their own questions/explanations. Use the latter to help get the discussion going.

2) <u>Problem:</u>   Transition from lecture to effective discussion seems most problematic part of a typical section, which is one reason I allow introduction to run too long.

   <u>Solution:</u>   Define specific questions during preparation and have them written down in full form.

3) <u>Problem:</u>   Questions and answers to students' questions tend to be too long.

   <u>Solution:</u>   Allow students time to respond — and give them time also to respond to each other.

4) <u>Problem:</u>   Unless students respond very positively of their own volition, I have a strong tendency to "fill in the gaps."

   <u>Solution:</u>   Must work on being confident that I don't need to "fill in the gaps" and can afford to (in fact would do better to) leave them the time they need to respond.

Developmental Issues

The case illustrated here is of an individual struggling with his first teaching experience. How will the videotape recall process work with a more experienced teacher? The long and short of it is: just as well, but in a different way. Research indicates that, "training that is cognitively more intrusive will likely be most helpful for the less able teacher; such intervention could disrupt the effective strategies of those more able" (Corno & Snow, 1986). The less able teacher may be more inexperienced and therefore have fewer concepts (for thinking about teaching) residing in long term memory. This, in turn, gives the teacher fewer concepts to access into short term memory from which new principles may be developed. In this case the consultant may find it most useful to focus on concept formation (the naming process).

A more experienced teacher most probably will have not only more concepts in long term memory, but a certain repertoire of principles to call into play as the situation arises. In this case, for the consultant to focus on concept formation will probably miss the mark. What may be more fruitful and palatable is a focus on developing a broader repertoire of principles for the teacher to *choose* from. Cues for taking this approach would be statements from the teacher at the beginning of the recall process that he or she may already have some focal points identified to address in the recall session. Here, the consultant may be wise to take a metacognitive approach and help the teacher learn to develop "reflection in action" (Schon, 1983).

Though some of the problems identified during the first recall session will also be seen during the second recall session, the consultant must remind the teacher (and himself or herself) that there had only been one hour of consultation influence on the teacher's behavior prior to that second recall session. I believe we have to maintain a realistic perspective and realize in most cases it will take more than one hour's consultation and a month's time to deal effectively with the kind of problems illustrated in this case example.

Here the teacher was still learning basic teaching skills about teaching a discussion section. The process of helping him develop principles of teaching to integrate those new skills in his teaching style will itself require "higher order skills," (Corno & Snow, 1986) involving making generalizations and transferring the knowledge gained in the consultation process to the classroom. These higher order skills are "metacognitive" (Shulman, 1986) in nature and may require a longer framework of time to develop. Indeed, the development of skills such as these is a lifetime process. To focus the teacher on a process of developing basic skills through creating an ever-growing repertoire of principles of teaching is itself a metacognitive process.

Given the complexities of the teaching situation and the psychological complexities of the videotape recall process for both consultant and teacher, I find that working from the recall/memory management framework can be very effective. In most cases I can see specific improvement even from the first to the second videotaping and this perception is equally shared by the teacher involved. The primary sources of data I have to support this statement are the completed recall forms of my clients (cognitive and affective indices) and their teaching behaviors comparing first and second videotapes (behavioral indices).

References

Allen, D.W. & Ryan, K. (1969). *Microteaching.* Reading, Mass: Addison-Wesley.

Ausubel, D.P., Novak, J.D. & Hanesian, H. (1978). *Educational psychology: A cognitive view.* New York: Holt, Rinehart & Winston.

Bellack, A.A., Hyman, R.T., Smith, F.L., Jr. & Kliebard, H.M. (1966). *The language of the classroom.* Final Report, USOE Cooperative Research Project, No 2023, NY Teachers College, Columbia University.

Bloom, B.S. (1953). Thought processes in lectures and discussions. *Journal of General Education, 7* (3), 160-169.

Carrol, J.G. (1976). *Effects of a teaching assistant training program on teaching behavior and student ratings of instruction.* Unpublished doctoral thesis, Cornell University, Ithaca, NY.

Clark, C.M. & Yinger, R.J. (1977). Research on teacher thinking. *Curriculum Inquiry, 7* (4), 279-304.

Corno, L. & Snow, R.E. (1986). Adapting teaching to individual differences among learners. In Wittrock, M.C. (Ed.). *Handbook of research on teaching,* 3rd ed. New York: MacMillan, 605-629.

Fuller, F.F. (1969). Concerns for teachers: A developmental conceptualization. *American Educational Research Journal, 6,* 207-226.

Gowin, D.B. (1981). *Educating.* Ithica, NY: Cornell University Press.

Joyce, B.(Ed.) (1979). *Education Research Quarterly. 3* (4), 6-99.

Kagan, N. (1975). *Interpersonal process recall: A method of influencing human interaction.* East Lansing, Michigan: Michigan State University, Dept. of Psychiatry.

Kagan, N. (1980). Influencing human interaction: Eighteen years with IPR. In Hess, A.K. *Psychotherapy supervision: Theory, research and practice.* New York: John Wiley & Sons, 262-283.

Kagan, N. (1987). Remark made at the annual meeting of the American Educational Research Association, Washington, D.C.

Leinhardt, G. (1983). Novice and expert knowledge of individual students' achievement. *Educational Psychologist, 18* (3), 165-179.

MacKay, D.A. & Marland, P. (1978). *Thought processes of teachers.* ERIC ED 151-328.

Novak, J.D. (1977). *A theory of education.* Ithica, N.Y.: Cornell University Press.

Nyquist, J.D. (1986). CIDR: A small service firm within a research university. *To improve the academy.* Professional & Organizational Development Network in Higher Education and National Council for Staff, Program and Organizational Development, 66.

Schank, R. & Abelson, R.P. (1977). *Scripts plans, goals and understanding: An inquiry into human knowledge structures.* Hillsdale, N.J.: Lawrence Erlbaum.

Schon, D. (1983). *The reflective practioner: How professionals think in action.* New York: Basic Books.

Shavelson, R.J. & Stern, P. (1981). Research on teachers' pedagogical thoughts, judgements, decisions and behavior. *Review of Educational Research, 51* (4), 455-498.

Shulman, L. (1986). Those who understand: Knowledge growth in teaching. *Educational Researcher, 15* (2), 13.

Shulman, L. (1987). Remark made at the annual meeting of the American Educational Research Association, Washington, D.C.

Taylor-Way, D. (1981). Adaptation of interpersonal process recall and a theory of educating for the improvement of college teaching. Paper presented at the annual meeting of the American Educational Research Association, Los Angeles.

Zeichner, K.M. (1983). Alternative paradigms of teacher education. *Journal of Teacher Education, 34* (3), 3-9.

David Taylor-Way is Director of Instructional Support at Cornell University. His academic background is in English/Photojournalism and Communication Arts and he has been in faculty development related activities since 1985. He welcomes comments and may be reached at the following address: Box 46, Roberts Hall, Cornell University, Ithaca, NY 14853, (607) 255-3493.

Appendix

Consultant's Leads for Use in Videotape Recall
(adapted from Kagan, 1975)

General:

Get in touch with thoughts, feelings, internal reactions

What were you thinking there?

What were you feeling there? What feelings did you have?

What kind of image were you aware of projecting?

Awareness Level:

Did you have a sense of how many people were with you?

Did you have any mental images at that point?

Did you have any bodily sensations at that point?

Verbal/Thought Congruence:

What did you want to ask? to say?

What were you trying to say? Did you say that the way you
wanted to say it?

Sharing Meaning:

Was it clear?

Did you know what he/she was leading up to?

What did (does) that mean to you?

Did you think he/she knew what you meant?

Was there anything (that you) left out?

What didn't you understand?

Did you know what he/she meant by that (statement of question)?

Does that make sense to you?

What did you mean by that?

Did that answer your question?

Feelings:

How were you feeling there?

Could you describe that (give an example of that)?

What made you feel that? realize that? gave you that impression?

How does that make you feel? (when that happens)

Did you have any feeling of familiarity, like "I've been through this before?" Where?

Were you aware of any risks involved here?

How did you think he/she/they felt about you?

How did you want him/her/them to feel?

Needs, Expectations, Wants:

What did you need/want from him/her/them?

Is there anything you wanted to say to him/her/them?

What did you want the other person to think (feel)?

Were there any imagined outcomes from that?

What did you think the consequences of that would be?

What did you expect him/her to think?

What did you think the other person wanted from you?

Conceptual Organization/Clarity:

Were the relationships between those concepts clear?

Could you summarize that (here in the recall session)?

What were the concepts you were dealing with here?

How accurately does the conceptual basis come across to you?

Teaching Strategy:

Did that (strategy) work?

What were you trying to do here?

What did you think he/she was trying to do?

What did you do about that?

Why did you decide to do that?

Is there another way out of that?

What were you trying to get at (with that question)?

What was your teaching strategy here?

Was that a good strategy?

Process:

How could you avoid that?

How could you have done that better?

Is that something you have control over?

What went wrong?

Why do you suppose that was (that happened)?

How did that happen?

What helped clear that up for you?

Do you know why you were doing that?

Discrepancies:

How does it seem to you now?

How do you see yourself now?

Do you like what you see?

Is that better (worse) than you thought at the time?

Do you agree with that?

Patterns:

How would you characterize (conceptualize) that?

Is there a pattern there in what you're seeing now?

Can you see any regularities?

Did you notice a pattern in what just happened (you just did)?

Were things going too fast (slow) here?

Teaching Principles:

What's a teaching principle you can generalize from that?

What do you conclude from that?

Could you summarize that?

Closure:

What has been of value to you from this recall session?

What have you learned today from this?

What are you going to take with you from this experience?

Part III:
Consultation for Professional Development

We are all aware that teaching is not the only responsibility which faculty members have in the university setting: there are also committee meetings, proposal writing, conducting research, writing of journal articles, and much more. Often, however, faculty development programs are not geared to assist faculty members in improving their performance in these other areas. This happens for a variety of reasons including a lack of training in areas such as career consulting or writing improvement techniques.

In the first paper in this section Wheeler describes a process used with faculty members who have doubts about their career choices. The main thrust of this process is clarification of issues which are involved in making career decisions and the gathering of information and data which will help the faculty member make a wise decision. The inclusion of sample questionnaires and an extensive bibliography make this article an excellent starting point for anyone interested in pursuing this area of individual consultation.

Writing proficiency is expected of all college and university faculty members but, just like teaching abilities, excellent writing skills are not a "given." In his program, Boice provides a series of workshops on improving writing and increasing writing productivity. The difference is that each workshop is followed by *field contacts* in which he visits with each participating faculty member in his/her office. During these visits he reassures, gives advice, and reinforces the use of helpful habits. He indicates that with the utilization of a structured approach even developers with little formal training as writers or as teachers of writing can conduct such programs.

By incorporating programs which focus on the personal and professional aspects of being a faculty member, faculty developers can do a lot to enhance the feeling of well-being which is so essential to the maintenance of job satisfaction in a stressful environment.

Career Consulting:
A Critical Segment of
A Comprehensive
Faculty Development Program

Daniel W. Wheeler
Teaching & Learning Center
University of Nebraska at Lincoln

Over the last eight years this consultant has interacted with many college and university faculty wrestling with career decisions. With the changing conditions in higher education of decreased mobility, an aging faculty, declining resources, and an unclear future, more faculty seem to be questioning the "One Life-One Career Imperative" so aptly described by Seymour Sarason (1977). As a result, for many faculty, making instructional improvements often does not address their more fundamental concerns about meaning and change of direction. This requires a deeper analysis which can be gained through career-life planning.

Unfortunately, few faculty developers have had training or focused experience in addressing career concerns. Far too often we are not prepared to help faculty clarify their doubts about their careers and help sort through career options. This chapter outlines a process to help faculty move on with their careers.

This process outlines individual diagnosis with a strong emphasis on clarification of issues involved in making career decisions and the importance of using compatible information-seeking strategies to obtain the information to make these decisions.

The Process

The Visible Groupings

Initially faculty usually fall into two career groups—those with a specific career issue and those with a need to address their whole career planning. The following examples show the differences in the two groupings:

1. Specific Issues:

   • Work Conditions (too much to do, conflict in the environment, non-supportive colleagues)
   • Consideration of an opportunity (different job or role)
   • Reactions to a change in the external value system (e.g., greater press for research)
   • Lack of a promotion
   • Tenure denial or termination

2. Career Planning Process:

   • Lack of a sense of the future
   • Dissatisfaction with whole work situation
   • Mismatch of skills and work

These two career groups are not mutually exclusive. Quite often a faculty member who comes with a specific issue such as an opportunity for a new role will start to explore the question of what that specific role will mean to their life as a professor. The more the issues are outlined, the more the faculty member finds a need to consider long-range goals and address strengths and weaknesses. The question may well become how does this opportunity fit into overall goals and interests which will require long-range planning.

Premise Underlying the Process

My basic premise is that the process of career consulting is rather pragmatic in that there are many activities and means to accomplish planning and no one method is best. If one activity or set of activities is not meaningful to a faculty member, then another should be substituted. The point is not to have faculty confuse methods with the process of career planning. For example, some faculty like the "nitty-gritty" procedures outlined in Bolles' (1975) transferable skill analysis while others find that process too tedious and would rather write biographical information from which to pull out their skills and abilities. Either method is fine if it gets skills out for analysis.

Role of the Consultant

The fundamental role of the career consultant is to help faculty assess their own situations and to help them take ownership for their growth. The consultation model used, defined by Wheeler and Mortensen (1984), is portrayed in **Figure 1**.

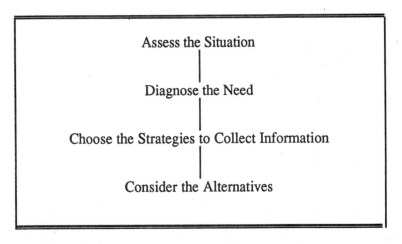

Assess the Situation

Diagnose the Need

Choose the Strategies to Collect Information

Consider the Alternatives

Figure 1. Model of consultant's role

From here we can further break down the phases of the model.

Assess the Situation

During assessment, the consultant asks questions, promotes self-analysis, and looks for cues. **Figure 2** shows the kinds of questions used to provide a reading on a faculty member's situation.

This assessment can sometimes be accomplished in one hour or hour and a half session. In some cases it may require more discussion after an initial period of reflection for the faculty member. An important cue is that if a faculty member shows little sense of career flexibility, the consultant needs to pay particular attention to barriers such as those listed in **Table 1**.

Question	Intent
•Describe your career at this point in your life.	•Self-Assessment •Looking for cues about barriers.
•What do you want to do? •How is it different from what you're doing now?	•Identify discrepancies •Identify sense of direction or lack of direction
•What do you see as your options?	•Assessment of present career flexibility

Figure 2. Questions to ask to assess situation.

As one can see from the listing, there are a number of potential barriers — some internal with the individual (for example, loss of purpose, powerlessness and internal values) and others external to the individual (for example, poor quality relationships and institutional practices). These factors

Table 1
Some Barriers in Career Consulting

1. **Poor quality relationships** with students, colleagues, and/or administrators. This includes poor communication and lack of respect.

2. A sense of **powerlessness.** It is particularly distressful to feel responsibility for whatever occurs, but perceive that you have little control over the outcome.

3. **Role Conflict.** Sometimes we feel pulled in different directions by the expectations of the community, clients/students, administrators, and our own personal philosophy, feelings, and thinking.

4. **Life Changes** external to the work situation. For example, events such as the death of a loved one, divorce or moving may diminish the energy and emotional strength that we bring to our work.

5. **Life Stages.** Adults continue to experience predictable life stages (passages) that decrease our capacity to deal with the emotional demands of our jobs.

6. **Internal Sources** of stress. Our ideas, values, and attitudes may cause us to experience stress in a situation that is not stressful to others.

7. **Institutional practices and policies** that foster competition and evaluation, and create situations that are likely to be stressful.

8. A **loss of purpose** or meaning in life; a lack of connection with others; a sense that the old assumptions don't work anymore.

9. **Total socialization to the profession** or the "One Life-One Career Imperative"; to consider any options would be a betrayal of commitment to "the chosen profession".

10. A sense of **entrapment**; there is nothing else I can do; my skills and abilities don't work anywhere else.

11. Need for **security**; a sense that to try something is a risk; it's better to hand on to what we have.

Expanded from Carol Payne, 1984.

can lead to a paralysis in which an individual will be frozen in time.

Another "tool" consultants may find useful to get a "fix" on faculty career is the **Professional Careers Checklist** (see appendix). This checklist helps to sort out where faculty members are along a continuum of career empowerment from a sense of no power to a sense of being at the top of one's career. People may want to make changes at any point on the continuum but a consultant needs to realize those feeling trapped and powerless will need more support and direction than those feeling well in control.

With these two activities, one can usually identify the factors that are limiting career growth. Some "barriers" require helping faculty look at their assumptions (for example, "the One Life-One Career Imperative") and breaking these down into manageable parts. Until this exploration and understanding of barriers occurs, faculty will not be able to move on to consider alternatives.

Diagnosis of the Need

After the assessment phase, the consultant needs to help the faculty member take ownership for what needs to be done. This requires an analysis of the benefits and limitations. Issues need to be clear and well defined.

For example, if a faculty member is feeling "trapped" and has no sense of the future, the consultant needs to help the faculty member see that some exploration is necessary to enlarge his or her perspective. Let's face it, a university can be a very limiting place if we allow it to be. It has always amazed me that faculty don't see this search for career development in the same light as a research problem in their area. If I can help them see their situation as such a problem, they can often go after it with the same intensity. "The Gaining New Information and Perspectives Sheet" developed in **Table 2** provides suggestions for strategies to address gathering information.

Table 2

Some Methods of Gaining Information

Method	Who Likes to Use	Remarks	Strengths
Experience -Internships -Practica	Clinicians and applied scientists	Emphasizes integrating knowledge with "real" situations	-Confronts assumptions & perspectives -Reinforces specific skills & identifies new ones
Informational Interviewing	"People" people (Extroverted, curious)	Quasi-research-interviewing often difficult for academics	-Provides personal information allows "reality" factor
Reading -Books -Articles -Technical Publications	The standby for academics	Introverted, abstract activity	-Much available, provides models as well as practical
Tests & Inventories -Strong-Campbell -Interest Inventory -Myers-Briggs Personality Inventory	Social scientists People "who believe in tests"	Many "hard" academics put no confidence in these instruments	-Can provide new areas to consider, confirmation of existing beliefs about interests & style or discrepancies to examine

(Con't on next page)

Table 2 (con't)

Method	Who Likes to Use	Remarks	Strengths
Trends Analysis -Census data -Occupational changes	"Data Projectors"	People who like to project in the future	-Provides continuous options to explore, provides a long-term sense of perspective
Writing -Journals -Biographies	"Creative Writers"	People who enjoy analysis & values clarification	-Allows getting ideas & feelings out where they can be examined, provides an historical record for perspective

Choosing Strategies

Choice of strategies requires having a repertoire of alternatives available. Differences in learning style and other personal learning considerations of faculty clients will form the basis for choosing consulting strategies. Some examples of strategies to address particular needs are given in **Figure 3**.

In addition, **Table 2** describes a number of methods for collecting information to make decisions. For example, a number of academicians exclusively rely on information gained through written materials while many "practitioners" rely extensively on experience and "informational interviewing." An important objective is to help clients see the value of using a variety of methods and the hazards of overdependence on any one of these techniques.

As you can see from the listing in **Table 2**, there are a variety of ways of getting the necessary information and the consultant needs to stay sensitive to helping faculty find the appropriate ones.

To this point a process with a number of suggestions for addressing career issues has been outlined. It has centered around the need for diagnosis and the searching out of needed information to make decisions. Now the career consultation process is followed through a case study with a faculty member.

A Case Study

The Contact

Most of my contacts come from direct calls from faculty asking for specific help or through referrals from fellow faculty, other faculty consultants, or administrators. In the case of Professor Talent, he called me one day and indicated that he had a great deal of stress related to his work. He said that he would like to find some way to get a handle on it "before it ate him up."

Career Issue	Strategies
•Having a sense of career alternatives	•Career testing - Interest and aptitude tests and inventories •Informational interviewing •Self-assessment of skills
•Work overload — Inability to say "NO"	•Set priorities in terms of goals •Learn to be more assertive •Educate "key decision-makers" to your priorities

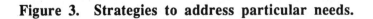

Figure 3. Strategies to address particular needs.

As soon as we set a time for an appointment, which needed to be as soon as possible to provide him some "peace of mind," I reflected upon his role and his departmental context. I knew his department had a long history of personal antagonisms and lack of cohesiveness. It is a small department with a strong sense of organizational vulnerability in which people were constantly "winning" at others' expense. I thought for the "toughest" of faculty this would be a most difficult environment in which to survive!

First Meeting

Professor Talent came to an appointment at 9:00 a.m. the next morning. I had never met him but had heard that he was a most creative fellow. When he entered my office, Professor Talent was nervous and hyperventilating. My first task was to help him deal with his stress level before we could address issues he wanted to address.

I mentioned that he needed to get a handle on the stress before we could get on to other aspects. Professor Talent immediately volunteered that he had been to the Counseling Center and they taught him a deep breathing exercise for the management of stress. I encouraged him to use this technique during our appointment and we would just gradually move into his situation.

As Professor Talent described his academic and personal life, he projected an image of never being able to say no and a tremendous sense of frustration that no one in his department would get involved in his projects. For example, he wrote grants which were funded and still couldn't get people to participate in the activities.

Assessing the Situation

Our first task was to break the problem down into manageable parts. It was obvious that Professor Talent needed some useful short-term stress management techniques to get some immediate relief. We discussed that he would continue to use the deep breathing relaxation techniques as well as look at the possibility of short walks each day (this would help release accumulated stress). We also discussed the possibility of keeping a daily journal in which he could write about his feelings and frustrations. This would offer a way to get these thoughts and feelings out.

Beyond these techniques, I suggested to Professor Talent that we needed to get a handle on the "stressors" and that he would need to make some decisions about them. I asked him to begin in this session and then to continue outside of this meeting to put down what he liked about his work and what he didn't like. I indicated that we would discuss these items next time and see if we could identify any major stressors. Immediately Professor Talent indicated the negativism in his department as a major stressor. We discussed that for a while and then I suggested he take "the assignment" with him and complete his task.

In this exercise I was working to identify how much of his dislikes were tied to conditions of work rather than the nature of the work. It was also quite apparent at this point that Professor Talent needed direct support, so we decided to meet weekly and that he should call me if he needed to touch base on managing the stress.

Second Meeting

The Diagnosis

Professor Talent called me only once this past week to ask about the assignment even though I think he probably just wanted to make contact. When Professor Talent came in, he appeared considerably more relaxed. I asked how his week had gone and he indicated that he only had one day when things really got to him. However, he found the stress management techniques kept it from getting out of hand.

When I asked about his "assignment," Professor Talent indicated that he wasn't sure what he found out. When I asked him to talk about what he liked and didn't like, he described the nature of his work as something he liked a great deal. What he described he didn't like were the conditions — lack of teamwork, sniping colleagues, lack of support for his work, and sense of departmental vulnerability to cuts and retrenchment.

During this conversation Professor Talent seemed relieved just to talk about these issues and to describe how much they wore upon him. We were both struck, as is sometimes the case in academic situations, that he liked the work but disliked the conditions under which he worked. In examining his stress resulting from an overload of responsibilities (brought on by his inability to say no) and the conditions of his work, our diagnosis was that he needed to establish his career priorities and address the work conditions that created much of the unwanted stress.

Strategies

What strategies could he use to address these concerns? We identified two avenues of action for Professor Talent. The first was what could he do in the department to improve his work conditions. Here we discussed activities such as: sitting down and discussing his career direction with the Department Chair and the Dean (he perceived the Dean was supportive but questioned the Chair's support); carving out his own niche and just going his own way; pairing up with someone he would enjoy in the department (no one fit the bill); and working with colleagues in associated departments or outside the university.

The second aspect was information gathering to find out whether conditions were different at other universities. I suggested he systematically collect these data through his conference attendance (talking to colleagues there) and engaging others in other universities in conversation when opportunities arose (for example, telephone contacts).

As part of the first direction, we discussed the need to establish some priority about work activities. Professor Talent indicated that he just couldn't say no and kept taking on responsibilities. In our discussions and in those with the college and departmental administrators, we decided to focus on establishing priorities. Our long-term objective was to establish these priorities so that Professor Talent could systematically "let go" of some activities and consolidate his energies.

The Information Gathering Activities

Over the next month (during a semester break), Professor Talent spent time setting some personal priorities through our discussions. He also did have conversations with the Dean and Department Chair. He found the Dean to be supportive and to provide some direction. Professor Talent didn't receive any specific help from the Department Chair. He concluded his activities and skills were not appreciated in this department. Although Professor Talent found it difficult to have these conversations with administrators and he didn't particularly like the results, he did find them useful in providing a baseline of information for decisions.

Considering Other Alternatives

During the same time period Professor Talent attended an important national convention and worked on a national steering committee for an upcoming conference. In his discussions there he found that there were other universities looking for faculty with his interests and skills. It was at this point that he decided he was going to seriously pursue "floating his credentials" to test his value outside his immediate department.

Continued Meetings

Professor Talent and I met approximately every two weeks over the next three months. We discussed how his outside search was progressing. We also discussed, given his departmental priorities, which activities he had dropped. In two cases he just announced that he would no longer do a particular activity. He found it stressful but was relieved after he did it. In one case a colleague picked up on the activity and in the other it just fell by the wayside.

In his priority setting Professor Talent was finding that his value system and interests just weren't of priority in his department. He was working to clarify the work context and even though he was handling the stress better, he was finding the work conditions were not becoming more enabling and weren't likely to change.

At about this time Professor Talent was invited for an interview at a large state university. He went to the interview and found that they were looking for a person with his interests and skills. He was offered, as part of the job, a number of facilities and materials he didn't have as part of his present appointment. He was offered more money. However, the telling factor for Professor Talent was that the department wanted his skills because they were integral to the college's work.

When Professor Talent returned from his interview, he came to see me about his offer. We discussed the advantages and disadvantages. I asked him to reflect on our conversation about work conditions and to see how that fit with his assessment of his potential. He indicated that it was a close fit. However, he was agonizing over leaving friends, disrupting family, and the uncertainty over what it would really be like in the new setting. I suggested he go home, think it over, and then give me a call. I also suggested one alternative was that he could bring his spouse to our next meeting. If he wanted, I indicated we could certainly discuss it further.

Two days later Professor Talent called to tell me he had taken the job. He just couldn't turn it down. I suggested it would provide him an opportunity to lay out his priorities and then make decisions around those priorities. Hopefully with this clarity of purpose and stress reduction techniques he would be better prepared to handle the new situation.

Postscript

It's unfortunate for our university that Professor Talent left. However, he seems to have found a better "fit" in terms of how he is integrated into the department and the work conditions are more conducive. One must also keep in mind that a continued association may well have created difficulties for both Professor Talent and the university. There could have been a turnabout but the stress of the environment might have also overwhelmed Professor Talent.

Discussion

Professor Talent is an example of difficulties which were focused on the conditions of the work. The situation may seem atypical or extreme. However, my experience is that the only part that was unusual involved the amount of time and support needed by Professor Talent because of his inability to sort out priorities. Generally, once the priorities and direction are set, academics will usually carry out the needed information gathering and exploration with little help.

Conclusion

Given the changing conditions in higher education and the "straightjacket" career model of many faculty, faculty development consultants should provide some activities for career clarification. At the very least, they should be aware of the kinds of career issues that surface and have a referral system (for example, counseling center, employee assistance center, or independent career counselor) to help faculty. I do believe that by using the suggestions outlined, a faculty development consultant can help faculty members sort out their concerns and find ways to move on with their careers.

References

Bolles, R. (1975). *What color is your parachute?* Berkeley, CA: Ten Speed Press, 182-218.

Sarason, S.B. (1977). *Work, aging,,and social change.* New York, NY: The Free Press.

Smith, C.P. (1982). *Taking care of ourselves.* Presentation at the Professional and Organizational Development (POD) Network in Higher Education National Conference, October 1982.

Wheeler, D. & Mortensen, L. (1984). Career and instructional consulting with higher education faculty. *To improve the academy, 3*, Professional and Organizational Development Network in Higher Education, 73-80.

Additional Reading

Bergquist, W. & Phillips, S. (1976, 1977, 1981). *A handbook for faculty development - Volumes I, II and III.* Washington, D.C.: Council of Independent Colleges.

Birn, A.G. & Kirm, M.O. (1978). *Life work planning.* New York: McGraw-Hill Co.

Bolles, R.N. (1978). *The three boxes of life.* Berkeley: Ten Speed Press.

Bridges, W. (1980). *Transitions: Making sense of life's changes.* Reading, MA: Addison-Wesley.

Donaldson, C. & Flynn, E. (1982). *Alternative careers for Ph.D.'s in the humanities: A selected bibliography.* New York: Modern Language Association of America.

Edgerton, R. & Baldwin, R. (1981). *Expanding faculty options: Career development projects at colleges and universities.* Washington, D.C.: American Association for Higher Education.

Figler, H. (1979). *The complete job-search handbook.* New York: Holt, Rinehart and Winston.

Furniss, W.T. (1981). *Reshaping faculty careers.* Washington, D.C.: American Council on Education.

Gilligan, C. (1982). *In a different voice.* Cambridge, MA: Howard Press.

Gould, R.L. (1978). *Transformations.* New York: Simon and Schuster.

Kaufman, H.G. (1982). *Professionals in search of work: Coping with the stress of job loss and underemployment.* New York: John Wiley and Sons.

Kirschenbaum, H. & Glaser, B. (1978). *Developing support groups: A manual for facilitators and participants.* LaJolla, CA: University Associates.

Levinson, D. **(with others)** (1978). *The seasons of a man's life.* New York: Alfred Knoph.

Lindsay, K. (1981). *Friends as family.* Boston, MA: Beacon Press.

O'Neil, N. & O'Neil, G. (1974). *Shifting gears: Finding security in a changing world.* New York: M. Evans and Co.

Patton, C.V. (1979). *Academia in transition: Mid-career change or early retirement.* Cambridge, MA: Abt Books.

Peshin, D. (1979). *A job loss survival manual.* New York: AMACOM.

Schein, E. (1978). *Career dynamics: Matching individual and organizational needs.* Reading, MA: Addison-Wesley.

Tough, A. (1982). *Intentional change.* Toronto: OISE.

Valillant, G.F. (1977). *Adaptation to life.* Boston: Little, Brown and Company.

Wyman, R. & Rissu, N. (1983). *Humanities Ph.D.'s and non-academic careers: A guide for faculty advisors.* Evanston, IL: Committee on Institutional Cooperation.

Zambrano, A. L. & Entine, A.D. (1976). *A guide to career alternatives for academics.* New Rochell, NY: Change Magazine Press.

Other Sources

Encyclopedia of Associations —Volumes I-V. Detroit, MI: Gale Research Company.

Newsletter About Life/Work Planning. Published six times a year by Richard Bolles, The National Career Development Project of United Ministries in Higher Education, P.O. Box 379, Walnut Creek, CA 94596.

Occupational Outlook Handbook. Washington, D.C.: U.S. Department of Labor Bulletin Annual.

Daniel W. Wheeler is a Staff Development Specialist at the University of Nebraska at Lincoln. His academic background is in Science Education and Curriculum Development and he has been in faculty development related activities since 1978. He has done career consulting with faculty from all the colleges and over 40 departments. He is also co-director of NUPROF — A Renewal and Redirection Project for Faculty in the College of Agriculture. For further information, contact him at : 221-A Ag Hall, University of Nebraska-Lincoln, Lincoln, NE 68583-0703. (402) 472-5558

Appendix

Professional Careers Checklist

How Would You Characterize Yourself?

___1. My career is really moving ahead. I'm quite satisfied.

___2. My career is progressing well, but I do want to explore some new avenues within my area.

___3. I'm satisfied with some aspects of my career, but I need to clarify my direction or means to achieve my goals.

___4. I'm feeling bored or unsatisfied with my career. I'm ready to pursue some new directions.

___5. I'm totally dissatisfied with my career. I dislike coming to work.

___6. I'm just starting a career. I want to get things in place and develop the necessary support.

___7. I've gotten to the point where I'm looking at retirement, but I'm unsure about the transition.

Professional Careers

Gaining New Information and Perspective Strategies

If an important issue in your career development is new perspective and additional information, then the following strategies and activities may aid in addressing their issues.

1. **Quite satisfied with my career choice — just want to pursue my present interests:**

   • Gather your resources to "make hay" while your interests and energy seem to converge with your professional image of yourself.

   • Build support for the future.

   • Do some long-range career planning while you are "on top of your game."

2. **Quite satisfied with my career — but do want to explore new avenues within my area:**

   • Attend a professional meeting "on the cutting edge" of your field.

   • Corner a "mover and shaker" in the field — "pick their brain."

   • Read some of the futurist literature — about trends and directions.

   • Subscribe to a journal in a potential area of interest.

   • Develop a grant proposal or team teach with someone in a related area (even
   a one-hour course).

3. **Satisfied with some aspects of my career — but want some aid in clarifying how to reach some of my career goals:**

   • Use some goal and value clarifying activities.

   • Talk with colleagues about strategies they use to achieve goals.

   • Design some activities to reach your goals — identify personal and professional support needed to achieve them.

4. **Feeling bored or unsatisfied with my career — ready for some ideas to pursue:**

   • Read some of the futurist literature.

   • Start a file of new ideas — articles, clippings, thoughts — review periodically for directions and possibilities.

- Attend workshops and conferences in a different or related interest area.
- Brainstorm ideas — evaluate later whether they are practical.
- Ask others how they see you in terms of careers.
- Do some "informational interviewing" of people in other areas to see if you
want to move into a new area.

5. Totally dissatisfied with my career — dislike even thinking about going to work:

- Sort out your feelings.
- Look at your options.
- Decide what you need to do to pursue options.
- Develop support to "move off-center."
- Recognize there is "risk" in doing nothing.

(A faculty member will probably need professional help, including counseling, with this state of affairs.)

6. Just starting on a career — I want to get it in place and develop the necessary support:

- Focus goals and support needed to achieve them.
- Analyze the system you're a part of.
- Establish priorities.
- Determine the kind of mentoring you want or need.

7. Considering retirement, but I am unsure about making the transition:

- Establish goals in retirement.
- Use resource people to examine the options.
- Deal with the necessary financial considerations —Social Security, TIAA-
CREF, living arrangements, other financial arrangements.

D. Wheeler, University of Nebraska

Glossary

career flexibility - The ability to define options. Anytime someone can define three or more, they are demonstrating flexibility.

career testing - The many tests and inventories used to help people sort out career possibilities. Two of the best known and most useful are the *Strong-Campbell Interest Test* and the *Myers-Briggs Personality Inventory*. Used solely by themselves, these tests can be misleading, but in conjunction with other information, they can provide powerful information.

informational interviewing - A technique in which one interviews others to gain information about work or careers in order to decide if one would want to pursue that work as a career.

"One Life — One Career Imperative" - Originally described by Seymour Sarason, this concept refers to "a calling" to a vocation to perform work that is seen as all-important and the only possibility in one's life.

transferable skills - Those skills identified in a present work situation that are usable in other work settings or careers. They are also sometimes referred to as "generic" skills. Examples would be organizing information, presenting information, and delegating responsibility.

Faculty Development Programs Based Around Scholarly Writing

Robert Boice
Center for Faculty Development
California State University, Long Beach

On most campuses, faculty receive no help for writing problems. Even where faculty development programs exist, scholarly writing is not targeted for change and faculty produce no more writing than would have occurred without the programs (Eble & McKeachie, 1985). Yet, scholarly writing grows in importance as a factor in hiring, promoting, and tenuring academicians (Astin & Bayer, 1979; Mahoney, 1979).

One reason we neglect writing may be a tendency, amidst some negativism about the overvaluation of publishing in academe, to forget two truisms about writing. The act of writing rewards those who do it (Boice & Jones, 1984) and disillusions those who don't (Austin & Gamson, 1983; Brace, 1968; Pellino, Blackburn & Boberg, 1984). Moreover, writing helps develop intellectual creativity in areas including teaching (Emig, 1981; Flower & Hayes, 1984; Hall, 1973; Weaver, 1982).

Another reason why faculty developers don't provide colleagues with more direct help in writing may be a lack of clear precedents in methods. This chapter is an attempt to provide one such precedent. It overviews formats that can produce meaningful and measurable increases in the output, comfort, and successes of faculty writers. And it suggests ways that developers with little formal training as writers or as teachers of writing can conduct such programs.

A Step-Wise Approach to Facilitating Scholarly Writing

The step-wise format of the essential program components presented here grew from trial and error experimentation over some 16 years (Boice, 1985b) and represents a series of tests of the efficacy of components (for example, Boice, 1985a).

The Dual-Locus Emphasis: Workshop and Field Contacts Combined

Rationale for the design. In my early workshops, I found that most participants were already writing; I had, for the most part, reached faculty least in need of help. That experience parallels a problem in traditional faculty development programs.

My follow-up questionnaires from those early workshops indicated that few of the participants persisted in their plans for changed writing habits; that is, writers already writing continued the same bad habits (for example, writing in binges) they brought into the workshop, and the few nonwriters continued the same habits (for example, procrastination, perfectionistic expectations) as before.

While workshops of this sort promote collegiality and provide inspiration, they seemed insufficient. Eventually I learned to add a more extended approach based around both workshops and field contacts.

This approach starts with a traditional *workshop*, but includes follow-up *field contacts* with faculty in their offices. In the field role, I reassure, give advice, and "reinforce" the use of helpful habits (for example, charting daily productivity in brief writing sessions). Data collected in these contexts showed that faculty with field contacts were far more likely to maintain the changes advocated in the workshop *and,* evidently, to produce both more writing and more satisfactions with writing thereafter. Where I (and where other faculty developers with whom I've worked) made individual contacts with faculty *both* before and after the workshop, the results were even more impressive.

In the preparatory stage of fieldwork, I selected a departmental unit as a whole and in collaboration with chairpeople made brief, collegial visits to all the faculty in that unit — always in faculty offices.

This anticipatory fieldwork consists of establishing rapport with all potential workshop participants, of requesting that each attend the workshop, and noting that attendance would be helpful to my research. (Faculty rarely refuse requests to be research subjects; moreover, this role provides them with a face-saving reason to participate.) I found that this pre-workshop fieldwork can increase the participation of "needy" faculty in developmental workshops.

Step 1:   Education/Demystification About the Writing Process

First workshop session. I typically begin the first in a series of hour-long workshops with an attempt to disabuse faculty about the myths that seem to inhibit productive and enjoyable writing. **Table 1** gives an abstract of the kinds of handouts I use in those workshops. This sort of handout, in my experience, becomes a lively topic of discussion that occupies much of the time allotted for this first, hour-long meeting. I present examples of my own workshop materials merely as suggestions; research on writing processes and on how academicians cope with them is, in my view, too primitive to permit anyone to claim a best approach.

One misbelief deserves special attention. Most faculty in my experience believe that *good writing requires large blocks of time;* most have learned to write in binges. Two problems in maintaining this belief are, first, that binging encourages procrastination (for example, waiting for that perfect, undisrupted day, vacation, sabbatical) and, second, that writing, if it occurs at all, occurs in fatiguing sessions were writing is neither enjoyable nor properly revised.

Table 1

Writing Workshop Handout:
Common Misbeliefs about Writing*

1. <u>Writing is inherently difficult</u>. In fact, good writing is no riskier and no less important than collegial conversation. Like speaking, writing does not need to be perfect to be effective and satisfying. But writing, more than speaking, offers a unique chance to "see what you think" and, in turn, to clarify your thinking.

2. <u>Good writing must be original</u>. In fact, little, if any, of what we think or write is truly original. What nonetheless makes "our" ideas worth communicating can lie in the novel ways we present them or in human frailty; readers can be retold even the most interesting ideas after a brief period of forgetting.

3. <u>Good writing must be perfect, preferably in a single draft</u>. In fact, the more successful the writer, the greater the likelihood that she/he revises manuscripts. And, in fact, successful authors are more likely to realize that perfect first drafts are perhaps undesirable.

4. <u>Good writing must be spontaneous</u>. This is the misbelief that writers should await inspiration. In fact, the most productive and satisfying way to write is habitually, regardless of mood or inspiration. Writers who overvalue spontaneity tend to postpone writing and, if they write at all, to work in binges that associate writing with fatigue. Writers who write regularly, in reasonable amounts, benefit in greater productivity and creativity.

5. <u>Good writing must proceed quickly</u>. Procrastination goes hand in hand with impatience. The very writers who delay writing often suppose that, properly done, writing must proceed quickly and effortlessly.

---

*An expanded version of this handout appears in Boice (1985d).

After discussing these Common Misbeliefs, I show the participants **Table 2**. The data in Table 2 (subsequent page) document two points: faculty members who have participated in this process showed higher levels of self-rated enjoyment with writing and of quantifiable outputs of writing when they abandoned binge writing and began writing in brief (for example, 30-minute), daily sessions.

Presentation of the data in Table 2 in workshops typically produces some surprise and disbelief. Some faculty even feel that some of their most cherished beliefs have been attacked. But the material depicted in Table 2 also generates new thinking on writing habits and induces some faculty to try changing them.

Table 2

Results with Selected Faculty who Switched, Post-Workshop, from Binge Writing to Writing in Brief, Daily Sessions*

Outcome Measure	Stage of Post-Workshop Writing Styles	
	Binge Writing (N=10)	Regular Writing(N=8)
Mean pages written per week	2.0	12.3
Mean self-rated satisfaction with writing	5.3	8.5

*"Binge" means writing on a minority of scheduled writing days and in sessions lasting longer than three hours; "Regular" means brief (30-60 minute), daily writing.

The remainder of this workshop, as I typically present it, deals with ways of finding a half-hour per day for writing in the midst of busy schedules. This is a critical point. Faculty need reminders that even during busy days they can pry loose a 30-minute period for writing. In fact, they can, according to hundreds of faculty I have "tracked" in direct observational studies. The most productive half-hour, evidently, lies in the start of the day. Writers generally work more efficiently and happily when fresh than in the evening. There is, in establishing such a schedule of brief sessions, an important lesson for academicians; it establishes writing as a high priority each working day but one that doesn't supersede other priorities such as teaching and socializing. There is also, in the reports of faculty who try this scheme, a second lesson: They learn that they can do "enough" writing (to publish one or two articles per year) to stop worrying about it and that writing no longer takes time away from evenings, weekends, and vacations.

But helping faculty find these times for writing is only part of the battle. They must also be convinced to try writing in sessions briefer than the big blocks of time they have learned to prefer. They suppose, initially at least, that thirty minutes is too little time to even warm up. One way to begin to change their minds is to practice brief writing sessions during workshops. Real changes in attitudes, however, come only with experience.

I also encourage participants to chart or graph their compliance with that schedule as a means of instilling motivation and of measuring progress. A typical graph consists of nothing more than time spent (or pages written) arrayed against scheduled writing days. Motivation comes in part from maintaining a "nice" graph of regular work and in part from the disappointment following occasional periods of inactivity.

Fieldwork following 1st workshop session. The fieldwork in this step has already been described. One aspect of the specific content of field visits (post-workshop), however, deserves more mention. In my experience and in that of other field developers I have helped train, individual meetings with faculty must address their resistance to change. That is, once faculty return from inspirational workshops to the realities of their offices, they often find excuses to resume old habits. Most such faculty, in my experience, need *direct coaching* on setting aside other (more habitual) activities, and on dealing with the impatience and other discomforts that well up when they face the prospect of writing in brief sessions (Boice, 1985a).

A typical example of faculty resistance illustrates the style that developers can take. This colleague, a new faculty member in his first year on campus, left the workshop feeling convinced that scheduling 30 minutes a day might help resolve his problems (i.e., feeling pressure but unproductive; worrying about surviving the tenure process; fearing that his prospects for professional success as a scholar were fading). Three days later when I visited his office, however, his mood had changed. Other commitments, especially demands to grade papers, had sidetracked his plans to write each weekday. Prospects of writing in half-hour sessions seemed silly. He even suggested that I was misleading faculty by telling them that they could manage writing on such a schedule.

What I did, first of all, was to ignore his unpleasantness; he was feeling frustrated. What I did next amounted to a bit of priming. I got him, while I sat and watched, to spend five minutes jotting down ideas that he could use in his next 30-minute session. Then I asked him to try to set aside his worries about finishing his grading tasks; thirty minutes wouldn't keep him from finishing the student papers. He agreed to try and to call me if he got stuck the next morning.

This colleague, like many others I've known, began slowly. It took a bit of practice to write without the luxury of warm-up time. My occasional visits to his office covered and recovered the same doubts. But by a few months later he had undergone a conversion experience; the regimen worked well. He was writing regularly, productively, and happily — without infringing on his other responsibilities.

Step 2: Spontaneity

Once colleagues find time for writing, they typically face other dilemmas about writing. As a rule, they need to learn more efficient ways of generating momentum and ideas, of establishing regular productivity, of making writing enjoyable, and of producing writing that is both public and publicly acceptable. Step 2, the procedure being discussed here, deals with the first of those.

Second workshop session. This session aims at little more than acquainting faculty with a procedure for getting writing started. The basic technique involved is most commonly known as free writing (Boice & Myers, 1986). Spontaneous methods of writing help coax writers to produce material freely, with a minimum of conscious interference. Elbow's (1973) instructions are clearest:

> The idea is simply to write for ten minutes (later on, perhaps fifteen or twenty). Don't stop for anything. Go quickly without rushing. Never stop to look back, to cross something out . . . to wonder what word or thought to use, or to think about what you are doing. If you can't think of a word or spelling, just use a squiggle or else write, 'I can't think of it.' Just put down something. (p.1)

I usually put Elbow's instructions at the head of an otherwise blank sheet of paper and, with little or no advance warning, ask all workshop participants to begin writing. Some of them look startled, but, in my experience, everyone including the most blocked writers begins writing almost immediately and produces at least several lines of writing. I ask participants to stop after only five minutes, in part because some writers will have filled their pages by that time.

Some curious things happen when colleagues are asked to stop writing at the five-minute mark. They resent being asked to stop; they share the belief of many writers that momentum, once established, should be maintained tenaciously. Another is the fear of public embarrassment that faculty expressed when asked to read their writing aloud. A third is the reluctant admission of each participant, once he or she has read aloud, that the quantity of writing produced is remarkable given the time span allowed and that the quality of at least some of the writing is surprisingly good.

As each participant reads his or her writing aloud, I ask other participants to make comments, preferably beginning with a specific compliment about what the listener liked. This exercise promotes several things foreign to many writers, especially those who have had trouble with writing: It emphasizes the positive in writing and helps show that effective writing need not be perfect. It encourages shared admissions that writing can be spontaneous, with little warm-up time, and can proceed quickly. And it helps make an ordinarily private (and often unnecessarily painful) act more public. Problem writers, in my experience, like to write in secrecy and are especially resistant to sharing early drafts of their writing.

Next, I have workshop participants try a second writing sheet, one with a slightly different format from that used for free writing. The point is to help writers produce spontaneous writing that is more on the track of scholarly prose. The instructions at the top of the sheet look like this:

Generative Writing Sheet I (GWS-1)

Pause just long enough to recall an experience from your school years that helped or hindered your writing. Then, before you've had a chance to think it all out, begin writing it spontaneously. Stick to the story, but don't stop for anything. Go quickly without rushing. Don't struggle over form or correctness. Just get something down. Keep it up for 10 minutes. [Actual worksheet has space for writing]

Here again, the writing proceeds with little discussion and all participants are asked to read, discuss, and support the results.

Then, before the same participants who complained earlier about the lack of generality from free writing to scholarly prose get a chance to resume that complaint, we proceed to the next approximation:

Generative Writing Sheet II (GWS-II)

Reflect briefly on a new writing project you'd like to develop. But don't reflect for long; you can always try another possibility in your next trial. Then begin writing. Go quickly if you have ideas readily available. Go slowly when you're thinking about directions, goals, audience, etc. But keep going. Don't struggle over form or correctness. Just make a beginning. Keep it up for at least 10 minutes; plan to do this exercise later for up to an hour if you're generating good, on-topic material. [Actual worksheet has space for writing]

And, finally, workshop participants try yet another extension of free writing. This task encourages writers to convert what they've already written into outline form and then back into more generative writing. The worksheet for this brief exposure to something that requires much more practice can follow this format:

Generative Writing Sheet III (GWS-III)

Generative writing may seem less chaotic, less pointless than spontaneous writing, but it still feels separated from real writing experiences. What comes next, then, helps facilitate the transition; it involves learning ways to transform generative writing into closer and closer approximations of a rough draft.

In GWS-III, I ask you to reread GWS-II and use it to generate a conceptual outline from what you've written. That is, sketch an informal diagram of the three or four main points that emerged (or would if you had written longer). The GWS-III format is intended *only* for a first approximation. You'll probably be more comfortable with your own, roomier work sheets. The important thing is to try it before you pause to recall how much you've always disliked outlining. [Actual worksheet has space for writing]

At the end of this workshop session I ask the participants to make actual plans for continuing this project. Colleagues are urged to plan sessions for writing and to estimate what they will be doing, outside the workshop, to extend their initial efforts at establishing a new manuscript. We spend a few minutes sharing these plans; this is a critical time for faculty to reassure each other that their beginnings at a manuscript are worth pursuing.

Fieldwork following 2nd workshop session. Most participants, in my experience, do follow through on the commitments they've made at the end of the Second Workshop Session to practice free writing and generative writing for 15-30 minutes a work day . . . at least for awhile. But many of the formerly unproductive writers continue to suspect that they are really wasting their time.

When I stop by the office of a participant for five to ten minutes during a scheduled writing time (these times are given to the field-worker at the end of the Second Workshop Session), I think that I help promote at least two aspects of writing. First, the prospect of my showing up seems to increase the likelihood of participants carrying out previously agreed-upon tasks. Second, I can help coach writers to continue to practice spontaneity while combatting the impatience that gets in the way of (a) working through preliminary stages and (b) of working in brief, daily sessions. Neither aspect of facilitating writing requires any special expertise in writing. I have found, however, that when I and other field-workers carry out similar regimens ourselves, our credibility and empathy seem enhanced.

Table 3 shows a sample comparison of participants in one of my own projects where some workshop participants agreed to follow-up visits and some did not. The data suggest that field visits (and, possibly, the willingness of participants to agree to such visits) make a substantial difference in promoting continuing involvement in the program.

Table 3

Long-Term Productivity and Satisfaction of Participants (N=24) With and Without Field Contacts

| | Outcome Measure | | | | | |
| | Writing Productivity (pages per week) | | | Self-Satisfaction with Writing | | |
Group	1 mo.	9 mo.	2 yr.	1 mo.	9 mo.	2 yr.
With field contacts	10.2	6.2	7.1	7.8	8.0	7.9
Without field contacts	6.5	2.2	1.5	7.8	6.7	6.1

Step 3: Regimen

Unproductive writers have difficulty believing it, but finding ways to establish momentum and to generate good copy are the easiest parts of the program. The more difficult parts, in my experience, involve maintaining momentum and turning it into finished and publicly communicated copy. Step 3 helps make writing regular and productive.

Third workshop session. This workshop tends more toward information than does the preceding one on spontaneity, but it seems to be most effective when experiential components are built in. The factual part consists of clarifying a series of commonsensical strategies that help increase the likelihood of writing occurring. **Table 4** lists some of these "externalized" principles.

Table 4

An Outline of Control Principles for Writing*

1. Establish one or a few *regular* places in which you will do *all* serious writing, places where you do nothing but serious writing.

2. Make regular writing sites sacred in the sense that no other temptations such as magazines, newspapers, novels can be on site.

3. Resist the temptation of doing other things first such as cleaning up one's writing site.

4. Arrange writing sites to minimize noisome distractions.

5. Limit social interruptions during writing times by:
   a) closing the door to your writing site;
   b) posting a writing schedule on your closed door that requests visitors to limit interruptions to brief (e.g., 10 seconds), essential messages;
   c) unplugging the phone; and
   d) enlisting significant others and colleagues as enforcers by asking them to help head off potential disruptions (including, of course, themselves).

6. Find another writer to join you for mutually quiet periods of work.

7. Make your writing site comfortable (e.g., write or hold the keyboard to a word processor in a recliner chair).

8. Make a more regular, recurrent activity (e.g., phone calls to friends) contingent on writing for a minimum period of time first.

Table 4 (con't)

9. Write while you're fresh. Schedule other, less mentally demanding tasks for times of the day when you're less alert and energetic.

10. Avoid writing in binges. Abandon the notion that writing is best done in large, undisrupted blocks of time. Waiting for such times does more than reinforce procrastination; it demands excessive warm-up times and it encourages you to write until you are fatigued.

11. Write in small, regular amounts; 30-minute sessions may be more than enough for most academicians.

12. Schedule writing tasks so that you plan to work on specific, finishable units of writing in each session.

13. Plan beyond daily goals. Schedule the stages of a manuscript in terms of weeks, again with specifiable and measurable goals so that you'll feel clear about where you're headed and about knowing when you've done enough.

14. Share your writing with supportive, constructive friends before you feel ready to go public. Ask your readers to appraise your writing in its imperfect and formative stages; they'll feel less judgmental and more inclined to offer advice for changes than they would with "finished" drafts.

Once workshop participants have this handout, they break into small groups where they role-play some of the practical and philosophical difficulties of putting these principles into practice. When the group re-forms as a whole, I find it helpful to

(a) encourage discussion of the difficulties in implementation, with participants supplying most of the suggestions for coping;

(b) illustrate the effectiveness of control procedures in producing regular productivity, especially with the use of contingency management; and

(c) anticipate reservations of participants about the creativity and quality of writing that occurs whether writers are inspired or not.

In my experience, some participants readily adopt the aspects of externalized procedures that prove helpful, while others cling to more traditionally humanistic approaches (Boice, 1985). The faculty developer presenting this workshop, so far as I can tell, functions more effectively by encouraging a diversity of views, by minimizing the conflict that can arise between them, by noting the value of talking about aspects of writing that usually remain private, and by advising discussants to keep an open mind for the experiences that can come via practicing externalized techniques.

Fieldwork following 3rd workshop session. At this point, the field contacts seem to be far more important than the workshop. As we saw in Table 3, faculty participants who maintained regular contact with a field developer were subsequently far more productive and satisfied as writers when they maintained these weekly follow-ups.

The content of these 10-15 minute field meetings as I conduct them is usually this:

1. start with small talk,

2. share charts of writing productivity (that is, preferably both participant's and field-worker's) and discuss distractions and other control-related problems in writing,

3. peruse participant's written pages and find some things that both the participant and field-worker can praise honestly, and

4. set specific writing goals for the coming week.

Here, too, no special expertise is required of the field-worker. He or she, in my experience, can function effectively merely by providing social support and reminders.

Where participants have questions about the quality of their writing, I typically encourage them to work through three steps. First, I ask them to be patient in developing a sense of "voice" in their writing by practicing generative writing daily, often in addition to more structured tasks under way. Second, I ask them to try revising manuscripts beyond the point where revision no longer seems necessary. Third, I ask them to share rough drafts with colleagues who receive specific requests for feedback about writing style.

In rare instances where concerns about writing skills persist, I enlist colleagues who teach composition to act as guides. They do so, in my experience, cheerfully and, as a rule, helpfully. But I caution participants about eliciting too much advice from these experts on writing. Composition teachers, as Elbow (1981) notes about his own kin, tend to be perfectionists and elitists who are often among the most blocked writers on campus.

Step 4: Optional Stages

Once programs are established, some faculty developers like to add one or more stages to those already mentioned.

Cognitive modification workshop. One such component deals with the discomfort that many writers continue to experience about writing, even when they are writing productively and successfully. The workshop format that I typically use to address this problem instructs participants in ways to observe and then modify their cognitions (that is, self-talk) about writing, particularly cognitions that generate anxiety and negative ideations. **Table 5** provides an example of the dysfunctional self-talk that accompanies writing prior to changes that come with simple exercises in cognitive modification.

The fieldwork for following up on the "Cognitive Modification Workshop" consists mainly of encouraging participants to continue practicing the journal-keeping and self-talk modification exercises begun in the workshop.

Social skills writing workshop. A second optional workshop helps ensure that faculty are successful in publishing or publicly circulating their writing. I typically label this

Table 5

Distribution of Participants' Maladaptive Cognitions (i.e., Self-Talk) at Scheduled Writing Times*

Category of Self-Talk	Percent of Sessions Where Cognition Was Listed	
	Blocked Writers (N = 40)	Productive Writers (N = 20)
Procrastination	90%	55%
Dysphoria/depression	77%	25%
Impatience	77%	35%
Perfectionism	69%	40%
Evaluation anxiety	32%	15%
Rigid rules	12%	10%

*Further details of this study appear in Boice (1985a).

workshop "social skills in writing." It emphasizes ways of making writing a more social and public act (e.g., arrange shared writing sessions with colleagues; circulating outlines and generative writing for collegial feedback), of coping adaptively with the editorial process (e.g., finding ways of defusing reviewers' comments and of learning from even the most discouraging criticisms), and of working toward a coherent and practical plan of writing. Here, as well as in other stages of these programs, I encourage colleagues to manage a productive schedule of writing while subjugating it to more important activities such as teaching and social life. I find the misbelief that writing, if it occurs successfully, must dominate a writer's life to be another powerful reason why many academicians resist writing.

The fieldwork for following up on the "Social Skills in Writing Workshop" helps perpetuate the process of coaching writers to stay on schedule and to practice plans for making writing more socially-skilled. I especially encourage them to contact me when they've just received an editorial letter. This is a time, in my experience, when participants who have received rejection notices feel like quitting. Advice on coping with such difficulties may be found in various sources including Scarr (1982).

Self assessment of writing difficulties. A third optional component provides self-assessments of the components of writers' difficulties with writing (e.g., impatience) and helps specify individualized ways in which to solve those problems. I use an empirically-derived but causal test, the Blocking Questionnaire (Boice, 1988), to prod writers into considering their attitudes and habits as writers. The Blocking Questionnaire encourages writers to compute their response scores into a profile compared to normative groups of academicians. These assessments provide useful material for discussion in both workshops and field visits. Moreover, the quantification in these indices helps writers check for changes in attitudes and habits over time.

Step 5: Making Missionaries of Participants

This last step consists of asking participants who have established steady records of productivity to enlist colleagues for mentoring in the same ways that they have been coached by the developer.

At least three benefits usually follow. First, the new faculty recruits usually benefit in the ways reported earlier in this paper. Second, all participants who enlist mentorees report the kind of understanding that comes only with teaching. And third, these efforts represent a step toward an ideal state of faculty development programs — one where the developer is no longer necessary.

Step 6: Dealing With Your Own Resistances

The most difficult aspect of sharing these ideas with other faculty developers comes in trying to convince them to implement a similar program on their own. While they often express real enthusiasm for my presentation of a sample workshop, they rarely see themselves doing subsequent workshops. They say something like this: "That was great. Why don't you come back and do the next workshop?" When I remind them of how much more effective the writing program will be if run by a faculty developer who conducts several workshops *and* carries out field visits, they give another standard response: "But I don't have the credibility you do."

Credibility, I then remind them, comes in workshop presentation much as it does in writing; the presenter must be willing to leap in and try it. It involves risks, especially public criticism. But it also involves learning. And it provides chances to help others (and oneself) in a difficult but rewarding aspect of academic life. Then I add a final point: There are few things, in my experience, for which faculty express gratitude as strongly as they do for getting help in transforming them into productive and happy writers.

References

Astin, H.S., & Bayer, A.E. (1979). Pervasive sex differences in the academic reward system: Scholarship, marriage, and what else? In D.R. Lewis & W.E. Becker (Eds.), *Academic rewards in higher education*. Cambridge, MA: Ballinger.

Austin, A.E., & Gamson, Z.F. (1983). *Academic workplace: New demands, heightened tensions*. Washington, D.C.: Association for the Study of Higher Education.

Boice, R. (1984). Reexamination of traditional emphases in faculty development. *Research in Higher Education, 21,* 195-209.

Boice, R. (1985a). Cognitive components of blocking. *Written Communication, 2,* 91-104.

Boice, R. (1985b). Psychotherapies for writing blocks. In M. Rose (Ed.), *When a writer can't write* . New York: Guilford.

Boice, R. (1988). The Blocking Questionnarie. Submitted to *Behaviour Research & Therapy*.

Boice, R., & Johnson, K. (1984). Perceptions of writing and publication amongst faculty at a doctoral degree granting university. *Research in Higher Education, 21,* 33-43.

Boice, R., & Jones, F. (1984). Why academicians don't write. *Journal of Higher Education, 55,* 567-582.

Boice, R., & Myers, P. (1986). Two parallel traditions: Automatic writing and free writing. *Written Communication, 3,* 471-490.

Brace, Gerald W. (1968). *The Department.*. New York: W.W. Norton.

Eble, K.E., & McKeachie, W.J. (1985). *Improving undergraduate education through faculty development.* San Francisco: Jossey-Bass.

Elbow, P. (1973). *Writing without teachers.* New York: Oxford University Press.

Elbow, P. (1981). *Writing with power.* New York: Oxford University Press.

Emig, J. (1981). Non-magical thinking. In C.H. Frederiksen & J.F. Dominic (Eds.), *Writing: Process, development and communication.* Hillsdale, NJ: Erlbaum.

Flower, L.S., & Hayes, J.R. (1984). Images, plans, and prose: The representation of meaning in writing. *Written Communication, 1,* 120-160.

Hall, D. (1973). *Writing well.* Boston: Little, Brown & Co.

Mahoney, M.J. (1979). Psychology of the scientist: An evaluative review. *Social Studies of Science, 9,* 349-375.

Pellino, G.R., Blackburn, R.T., & Boberg, A.L. (1984). The dimensions of academic scholarship: Faculty and administrator views. *Research in Higher Education, 20,* 103-115.

Scarr, S. (1982). An editor looks for the perfect manuscript. In D. Loeffler (Ed.), *Understanding the manuscript review process: Increasing the participation of women.*. Washington, D.C.: American Psychological Association.

Weaver, F.S. (1982). Teaching, writing, and developing. *Journal of Higher Education, 53,* 586-592.

***Robert Boice** is Director of the Center for Faculty Development, and Professor of Psychology at California State University, Long Beach. His* *academic background is in Psychology and he has been in faculty development related activities since 1978. He has published widely in areas including ethology, observational and clinical skills, writing, teaching, and faculty development. He has presented talks and workshops on faculty development at a variety of campuses. And he works as a clinical psychologist with blocked writers. He may be reached at: Faculty Development Center, California State University, Long Beach, Long Beach, CA 90840. (213) 498-5287*

"So You've Got Them in Your Office—Now What?"

(Some Conclusions)

Once, long ago, the original title of this volume suggested by its editor-in-chief was "So You've Got Them In Your Office—Now What?" Perhaps it is time to ask that question again. If "Them" is any given faculty member and if "Your Office" can mean almost anywhere on or off-campus, the chapters of *Face to Face* should help you answer "Now What?" Before we send you on your consulting way, let's conduct a review. To check out the "Now What?" you are invited to imagine yourself in the following scene.

It is nearly midmorning on a typical autumn day on your campus. You are in your office. You have just finished reading another selection from *Face to Face*. Putting the book down, you glance at the clock overhead. In one hour, you will grab a manila folder with a few sheets of paper in it, extract your jacket from the closet (frost is in the air), and dash across campus to meet with Professor—well, although the two of you have talked only once, you are already on a first name basis, so let's call her Linda. In this hour, minus a few minutes—how time flies—it is time to review what to do. Does your interior monologue as you prepare to meet Linda go like this?

"I really do not know much about Linda except her department and that she wants to see me. The staff directory lists her as an assistant professor and indicates that she is starting her fifth year on campus. Hmmm. I wonder if she is tenured? Probably not. Obviously, I need to find out a lot about Linda, but maybe I better ask her right away why she called me. I want to be sure to work on her agenda, not mine.

"Reminder: don't talk too much. Ask her questions, listen, probe, and summarize. Together we should state the issue or the problem—which, I also remind myself, does not necessarily mean she has a PROBLEM!

"I will be prepared to suggest how we might together work to address her concerns whatever they are. One thing I want to avoid is giving the quick fix. It is so expected. Our fellow faculty members are sharp. Make a brief suggestion, the light goes on, and off they go in a new direction—or so they think. So unless she asks me where to get overhead transparencies made, or some such question, no glib statements from this mouth! I want to be sure she knows that the process of analyzing teaching and making improvements needs to be systematically structured and that we need to gather information for me to be of assistance.

"Remember to tell her that working together also means that the information we collect is hers, that it is treated with confidentiality, and only she has the right to release information gathered by us.

"There, now that is straight in my head. If Linda does want to work on classroom instruction, I hope she's ready to get started right now. I do have time to schedule her in and there's sufficient time left in the semester to make modifications in the current course.

"What tools of data collection shall I use? No need to overdo it—alas, my tendency. We'll have the three perspectives: hers, mine, and the students. Precisely what tools are to be used I will have to wait until I talk with Linda to decide—only 45 minutes from now.

"Well, what do I have in my bag of tricks? *Face to Face* is helpful. I already pretty much know the questions I want to ask Linda to find out about her attitudes as a teacher and her views of her students. How we go about collecting student data is another issue. It's a little late for a student observer—maybe next semester. For now, I could use TABS or SGID. I should also think about using randomized students in discussion groups if she has general or undefined concerns.

"What about classroom observation? Perhaps I should use an objective observation system, such as Flanders or CIAS, and plan a sequence of coding behaviors, feedback, modification, and recoding. Then, again, a verbatim recording of what is happening is useful. Another choice I have is videotaping. In fact, either the objective observation system or videotape-recall could provide the main process for our work together.

"Oh, dear. I seem to have acquired an embarrassment of instructional improvement riches. After taking Linda's concerns into consideration, perhaps I better choose the method of data-gathering I am most comfortable with at the moment, and try out new methods on faculty colleagues I have worked with previously and are tolerant of my urges to experiment. After I give a little more thought to the rationale of one-to-one consultation and its strategies, I do plan to add to my repertoire of methods.

"Look at that clock! I'd better tell the secretary I am heading out and get going. Let's see, do I have copies of the description of our consulting services and individual work? My appointment book?—I can't forget that! Should I assemble my handouts now or wait until the next visit? I think I'll hold off on that for now—pull from my files once I have a better sense of who Linda is and what her concerns are. I should get a workshop flyer from the secretary on the way out, since I will probably want to invite Linda to one of our workshops. And while I am talking with the secretary, I'll get her to check on my plane ticket to POD.

"The air is certainly autumnal! Sudden thought. If Linda is not really concerned about teaching but more about tenure or her career, I'd better direct her to some of our resources on career planning and if appropriate, writer's block...."

Here the scene breaks off. Presumably, our peraumbulating consultant now enters the right building and knocks on Linda's office door. This review has been successful for us and for you if it triggered some thoughts on how you would prepare to meet a first-time faculty client. To check us out further, if you can persuade a colleague to be "Linda," the two of you might role play the ensuing conversation. How well were you prepared to talk to Linda? When you have finished the conversation, have you agreed upon the purpose of the consultation and the means and dates of collecting data, and the date of your next meeting? What are some issues, concerns, or feelings arising out of your initial meeting with Linda? How will you proceed from here?

One thing you may have noticed in the scene above—as well as in the descriptions in the various chapters in this book—is that the process of the consultation and the strategies for data-collection appear to take up a great deal of space. Very often, in fact, data-collection and feedback become the intervention. The reason for this emphasis, as I see it, is that we believe in the power of feedback combined with personal support. Change will occur when feedback is precise, clear, and focused and when the faculty member has someone — consultant or colleague — to work with. The models of instructional change described in this volume encourage a teacher to accept a diagnosis of current practices in his or her teaching and to develop some understanding of learning theory and strategies of instructional improvement and design. Most recommendations for improving teaching can be grouped in relatively few categories: organizing materials meaningfully and clearly, relating to students, improving classroom communication, designing equitable methods of testing and grading, and increasing active learning. The faculty member as the subject matter expert must ultimately make the precise application to the material. The consultant coaches, watches from the wings, and then (we hope) slips gracefully out of the picture.

Instructional consulting is a challenging task. Fortunately, with feedback and support, university teachers can make dramatic improvement in their students' perceptions of the course and instructor. This kind of change is perhaps the major reward those of us in faculty development and instructional improvement seek. There are other rewards as well. Because faculty developers often exist "on the margin," as Herman Blake described us once, we do not fit easily into traditional academic lines and structures. Although we often exist precariously, we also have the freedom to move across the disciplines, departments, and colleges almost at will. One day I may observe a class in introductory philosophy and the next I am watching a faculty member work with students in a clinical setting. This freedom of movement makes us uniquely able to sense the pulse of our campus and gives us special power to improve its climate for teaching and learning. And that's what this job is all about.

—Joyce T. Povlacs
Lincoln, Nebraska
May 2, 1988

Index